WISE
CHOICES

GOD'S WAY FOR ROMANCE

Getting back to biblical courtship

STUART BURGESS

Commendations

In a culture where transitory 'relationships' have become the norm and lifelong fidelity is spurned, this book offers hope that we can experience life in a richer dimension. The author shows us through incisive cultural criticism how we have cheapened true love and also gives us a range of compelling reasons why we should retain our purity until we marry. This is the book I will give to anyone who feels tempted to take the low road to finding true love and companionship.

Revd Peter Hastie, Principal, Presbyterian Theological College, Melbourne, Australia

Courageously frank, biblically clear and pastorally sensitive. This is much more than sound advice on 'courtship': it is a penetrating glimpse into the context of the downward spiral of morality among our young people today. Pastors and youth leaders, get it into the hands of your young people and use it for open discussion.

Brian Edwards, author and former pastor

I sincerely believe this excellent book will do much good among the young people of our churches. It has been a long time since a book was published on this theme that was so comprehensive and clear and yet at the same time written in such a considered and sensitive tone. I would have no hesitation in recommending it and using it among our own young people.

Roland Burrows, Pastor, Cradley Heath Strict Baptist Church, UK

While vividly presenting the deficiencies of a transitory-relationship culture, the author consistently upholds and pragmatically presents God's principles for marriage. May our children learn from this book to fear God and greatly delight in His commandments as they pursue His best for their lives.

Scot Chadwick, Pastor, Williamstown, Kentucky, USA

Today's secular worldview can be seen in the church. Dr Burgess plainly and biblically addresses an issue that the church is very confused about. I wholeheartedly recommend this book to anyone seeking God's way for a blessed marriage. I plan for my kids to read it.

Dr Andrew Fabich, Science professor, Liberty University, USA

I was so excited to read this book—it is so refreshing! It shows maturity, wisdom, deep scriptural understanding, excellent application and heart. The points are thoroughly supported with Scripture, statistics or anecdotes.

Rowina Seidler, Editor of 'Ruby in the Rough' online magazine

This book highlights just how alienated modern-day culture is from biblical teaching. It is so necessary in today's confused times. This much-needed book fills an obvious gap and I thoroughly recommend it.

Alec Taylor, author

A very helpful book relating to a vital area of the Christian life—a subject which has not been dealt with properly in the UK for a long time. We trust it will be of great help to young believers seeking to honour the Lord in a godless world.

Bill Goodman, Pastor, Bethel Chapel, Bath, UK

If, like me, you grew up in the 1980s–1990s or later, you will have little idea of how the 'relationship culture' has invaded every aspect of our lives, and of the danger it brings. We have a desperate need to return to God's ways and to understand what the Bible teaches about how to approach marriage. In this short book Stuart helps us do this as he combines his academic precision with a pastor's heart. I wish I had read this book when I was a teenager!

Jonathan Hunt, Pastor, Morton Baptist Church, Bristol, UK

© Day One Publications 2016

First printed 2016

ISBN 978-1-84625-497-0

British Library Cataloguing in Publication Data available

Published by Day One Publications, Ryelands Road, Leominster, HR6 8NZ

Telephone 01568 613 740 FAX 01568 611 473

email—sales@dayone.co.uk

web site—www.dayone.co.uk

Cover design by Rob Jones, Elk Design

Printed by TJ International

For my wonderful wife,
who had a very significant input
into every chapter of this book.

Acknowledgements

I am grateful to many people for the discussions I have had with them and for their comments on this book, including Roland Burrows, Brian Edwards, Guy Davies, Alec Taylor, Philip Taylor, Chris Boyes, Susan Stone, David Carron, Ben Osterkamp and Rowina Seidler. I am also thankful to numerous students for their feedback, as well as to my wife and children, who gave very helpful comments.

Contents

Foreword

'Relationship' is now used to describe almost anything—from an association with a work colleague, through a nodding acquaintance with a neighbour, to a romantic relationship. Thus it should not surprise us that the concept of a 'relationship' usually implies nothing more in the modern world than a passing arrangement. However, it was not always like this. It was characteristic of life in a bygone age that the concept of a relationship had great sanctity and significance.

One of these relationships was marriage—the deepest of our personal associations. Marriage is secured by a solemn and special agreement known as a 'covenant' (Mal. 2:14). In Scripture a covenant is a sacred bond that carries life-and-death implications for those who pledge themselves to it. It is significant because it was the instrument that God used when He wanted to remind His people that they had a secure and inviolable relationship with Him (Ezek. 16:8). Marriage implies permanence, faithfulness and undying love.

Naturally, it is only when we realize that marriage is a covenant that we understand that there is more to this relationship than personal fulfilment. It involves a lifelong pledge that is modelled upon God's persevering love for His people. And it is in this union of ultimate commitment that we discover true joy and lasting pleasure. Casual relationships have never been able to deliver the delight and contentment that come through the security and sanctions of marriage.

And this is the point of this book. It reminds us that, since marriage is the goal, the means by which we pursue it must be consistent with the ideals of marriage itself—and that includes personal purity and faithfulness before marriage.

I think this book will appeal to many in the younger generation because it is short on moralizing but provides many convincing reasons as to why we should pursue the ideal of courtship rather than take the low road of having sexual intimacy before marriage. It is written in a simple yet elegant style that builds a compelling case through convincing and cumulative arguments. That's a gift for any counsellor! I strongly recommend it.

Revd Peter Hastie,
Principal, Presbyterian Theological College, Melbourne, Australia

Preface

The purpose of this book is to explain what the Bible teaches about purity before marriage and to explain the dangers of the modern relationship culture. We live in a society where there is great peer pressure to have sexually intimate relationships before marriage, and that peer pressure has entered the church. There is a burning need for Christians to be aware of biblical principles relating to courtship and dating.

I know many people in the UK and USA who have saved themselves for marriage and have been blessed both before and during marriage. I have also seen first-hand the harmful effects of the relationship culture. In my roles as Head of Department and Senior Tutor in a university department with around five hundred students I have often had to deal with students with serious relationship problems. And in my church ministry I have seen some Christians suffer the same harmful consequences of relationships.

If any reader has a history of intimate relationships outside of marriage either before or after becoming a Christian, it is important to know that there is complete forgiveness and healing through the Lord Jesus. It is also important to know that it is never too late to change lifestyle. I know many people who, with God's help, have turned away from the relationship culture and known the blessings that follow. Avoiding intimate relationships outside of marriage can be one of the most important decisions a person makes in his or her life.

This book is written not just for single people but also for parents and church workers who want to promote biblical standards of conduct in courtship and want to see godliness in the church. It is hard to find books on courtship that really focus on what the Bible teaches in this area. I have endeavoured to search out every important biblical principle relevant to courtship.

The battle for purity in courtship is one of the most important spiritual battles facing the church today. Courtship is an area in which it is vital for Christians to walk by faith, trusting in the commands and promises of Scripture. Church history shows that when God brings about revival, there is often increased godliness among God's people. If young people turn away from the relationship culture, that could play a part in the revival of the church.

Introduction

Choosing a spouse is one of the most important decisions a person can make in life, with far-reaching consequences. It is therefore vitally important to follow the Bible's teaching about purity and marriage. In the area of courtship we can choose God's way or the world's way.

1. God's way: save your heart and body for marriage

At first sight it might appear that the Bible is silent on courtship and dating. However, the Bible gives extensive teaching on the subjects of marriage, divorce and sexual purity, all of which is very relevant to courtship. From this teaching it is clear that God has designed lifelong marriage as the only way for two people legitimately to belong to each other and have sexual intimacy. And God has designed lifelong marriage as the only way for a man and woman to have romantic fulfilment.

Since intimacy should be saved for marriage, it directly follows that the purpose of courting should be to investigate the possibility of marriage and not for two people to be joined together as a couple. In other words, courtship is a means to an end (to consider marriage) and not an end in itself (to have a sexual relationship). Of course, going out with someone can involve powerful feelings of attraction, but it should not involve two people giving their hearts and bodies to each other.

There are many blessings in saving yourself for marriage. The blessings include a greater likelihood of finding a godly spouse and a greater likelihood of having a happy marriage. There is also the joy of giving the gift of purity (or a period of staying pure) on one's wedding day. For Christians who stay single, life is happier and godlier when they have avoided intimate relationships.

2. The world's way: don't save yourself for marriage

Modern society rejects the biblical principle of staying sexually pure before marriage. There is now what can be termed a 'relationship culture', in which people are expected to have a series of non-permanent relationships from a very young age. The Christian author Paul Webster has described modern relationships as 'recreational dating'. This term illustrates how dating is pursued for pleasure rather than as a means for choosing a spouse.

The fact that modern society has replaced the term 'courtship' with 'relationships' helps to illustrate how society has rejected the biblical principle of saving your heart and body for marriage. Whereas 'courtship' means that two people are courting the possibility of marriage, the term 'relationship' means that two people *do already* have a type of marriage relationship. Whereas the term 'courtship' means that people do not yet have permission for sexual intimacy, the term 'relationship' means that two people *do* have permission (in the eyes of modern society) to have sexual intimacy. Of course, not everyone who says he or she is 'in a relationship' has given his or her heart and body away. However, in modern society the term 'relationship' is taken to mean an intimate sexual relationship.

There is now a great contrast with past societies that respected biblical teaching on marriage and purity. Whereas in past ages all intimate relationships outside of marriage were considered illicit, modern society teaches that all intimate relationships are fine as long as they involve two people who are above the age of consent. Even the education system now promotes the relationship culture through sex education. The whole basis of Sex and Relationships Education (SRE) in schools is the assumption that sex and relationships are fine outside of marriage.

The Bible warns that having sex and relationships outside of marriage has harmful consequences. Relationships inevitably lead to serious problems because they go against God's design for romance. Relationships are one of the main reasons why people have problems such as emotional trauma, unstable lives, unwanted pregnancies and sexual diseases. I have seen many young people go through painful experiences as a result of having relationships.

The relationship culture is also harmful to the institution of marriage because it is an alternative to marriage. People say they don't need to marry or can delay marriage because relationships give them permission to have sex and romance outside of marriage. Relationships are also a major reason why divorce rates have increased dramatically over the last fifty years. The relationship culture makes people think that 'splitting up' is normal and acceptable, and they take that philosophy into marriage.

Sadly, the relationship culture has been gradually creeping into the church. There are Christians who think it is fine to have relationships with a degree of sexual intimacy and to go through relationship splits. Such Christians inevitably experience the devastating consequences of relationship splits.

3. Choosing God's way with God's help

It is not easy to preserve purity before marriage in today's lust-filled culture. However, God knows the challenges facing Christians today and He is ready and able to help them follow the right path. God's grace is sufficient for all the challenges that we face today in the relationship culture. God's Word is also all-sufficient for guiding us in every decision we make in life. To follow a pure lifestyle is hard in the short term, but in the long term there are many blessings that will come.

IT IS IMPORTANT
TO REALIZE THAT
ENTERTAINMENT IS
MUCH MORE THAN
JUST ENTERTAINMENT.
EVERY DAY PEOPLE
ARE BEING TAUGHT
MORAL STANDARDS
THROUGH WHAT THEY
SEE AND HEAR IN FILM,
TELEVISION, POP MUSIC
AND MAGAZINES.

1. The world's way: the relationship culture

Key biblical principle: LUST IS SINFUL (MATT. 5:28)

Jesus taught that when a man looks with sexual desires at a woman who is not his wife he is guilty of the sin of lust. The reason it is sinful is that he is not married to the woman and so he has no right to imagine sexual activity with her. This key teaching of Jesus' is equally true when a man has sexual desires for a woman who is his girlfriend. When a man looks at his girlfriend with sexual desires or touches her in a sexual way it still represents the sin of lust. The reason it still represents lust is that the two people are not married and there is no lifelong covenantal commitment between them. The fact that a woman may be happy for her boyfriend to touch her in a sexual way (and vice versa) does not make it morally acceptable for sexual touching to take place. Jesus never said that 'it is wrong for a man to lust except for the case where a woman gives consent for a man to lust after her'. Of course, courtship involves strong attractions and a strong desire for marriage, but courtship does not give permission for sexual intimacy or sexual desires.

Over the last hundred years there has been a gradual rejection of biblical teaching on sexual morality. Before 1900 society generally accepted the biblical teaching that lust is sinful. If women dressed in seductive clothing it was generally considered immoral because they were encouraging men to look lustfully at them.

Of course, society was far from perfect before 1900, with a minority of people having mistresses or using prostitutes. However, the key point is that past societies did not approve of lust or sexual immorality because of biblical teaching. The difference today is that society approves of lust and rejects biblical standards.

A key change over the last hundred years has been that courtship has changed from being a means to investigate marriage to something that is pursued for pleasure. In modern society there is great peer pressure to have intimate relationships from a young age regardless of whether there is an interest in marriage or even an ability to marry.

One of the main reasons why society has rejected biblical standards over the last hundred years is that the entertainment industry has replaced the Bible as the place where most people learn their moral standards. The entertainment industry teaches that it is fine to dress seductively and to look lustfully at other people. It teaches that it is fine for people to give their hearts and bodies away in sexual relationships before marriage.

It is important to realize that entertainment is much more than just entertainment. Every day people are being taught moral standards through what they see and hear in film, television, pop music and magazines. Many studies have shown that people are quick to copy the standards they see in entertainment such as film and television. As a result of the world's entertainment, we now live in a lust-filled society which approves of all kinds of sexual immorality.

This chapter gives an overview of how the entertainment industry has been instrumental in the development of the relationship culture over the last hundred years.

1. The growth of the relationship culture in the film industry
In July 2011 I had the honour of being invited to be the orator at Bristol University for the award of an honorary degree to Ben Morris for his Oscar-winning animation work in films such as *Troy* and *Gladiator*. Like most people I really enjoy watching a good film, but I find it sad that so many modern films have immoral sexual content.

The global entertainment industry can be considered to have started in the early 1900s, which is when the film industry was born. Right at the start of the film industry, producers knew that immoral sexual content is a powerful way of getting higher ratings and money. Human nature is such that films with the most sexual content will tend to attract the biggest audiences and make the most money.

A clear pattern can be seen of moral boundaries being pushed to make films more appealing, especially among younger people. After a few years the immoral practices are seen as acceptable and are copied by society. Then the producers push the boundaries a little further to keep making money. We can identify the following key milestones in the film industry of pushing the boundaries of sexual content:

MILESTONES OF SEXUAL CONTENT

1915 *A Fool There Was*. Theda Bara was one of the first 'sex symbols'.

1926 *The Temptress*. The first Hollywood film with an open-mouthed kiss.

1927 *It* (Paramount films). Twenty-two-year-old Clara Bow became a sex symbol.

1943 *The Outlaw*. Jane Russell became a sex symbol after dressing seductively.

1962 *Dr No* (James Bond). Glamorized casual sexual encounters.

1966 *One Million Years BC*. Made Raquel Welch a sex symbol.

1972 *Deep Throat*. The first pornographic film watched widely.

1990 Obsession with relationships in films (*Titanic*, 1997 and *American Pie*, 1999).

1998 *Gia*. Film promoting a lesbian relationship, starring Angelina Jolie.

2010 *The Karate Kid*. Film showing twelve-year-old children kissing.[1]

The milestones listed above show how there has been a gradual but large drop in standards of sexual morality over the last hundred years. The emergence of sex symbols in 1915 encouraged society to view lust as morally fine. The introduction of kissing scenes in 1926 encouraged society to view a degree of sexual intimacy outside of marriage as morally fine. The sexual revolution of the 1960s promoted sexual intimacy outside of marriage as morally acceptable. Since the 1960s the phrase 'being in a relationship' has emerged to emphasize that sexual intimacy is considered normal outside of marriage.

When certain behaviours are acted out by popular actors, this speeds up the adoption of that practice by society. When Clark Gable had an intimate kiss with Movita Castaneda in the film *Mutiny on the Bounty* (1935), it reinforced society's acceptance of intimate kissing outside of marriage. When Angelina Jolie acted out a lesbian role in the film *Gia* (1998), that had the effect of making society see homosexuality as morally acceptable.

The fact that famous actors often lead immoral lifestyles has further accelerated the moral decline in Western society because people inevitably copy the behaviour of their idols. Famous actors in the twentieth century, such as Clara Bow, Marlon Brando, Clark Gable, Richard Burton and Elizabeth Taylor, had serial divorces and relationships in their lives and that has made society more accepting of divorce and relationships. The vast majority of current famous actors have serial relationships, so that is what society now sees as morally acceptable.

One of the most influential films in the 1960s was the first James Bond film, *Dr No* (1962). While Bond films contain much innocent action drama, they also contain immoral sex scenes involving casual sexual behaviour outside of marriage. In the 2012 Bond film *Skyfall* there is a sex scene in a shower that is shown in the main trailer of the film, showing that sex is an important selling point of James Bond films. In many modern films, producers will deliberately include one or two explicit sex scenes in order to make their films popular.

One of the features of films since the 1990s is a focus on romantic relationships outside of marriage. In most modern films the storyline centres on the development of various romantic relationships and these generally include sex outside of marriage. Even films about historical events are now just as much about romance as history. In *Titanic* (1997) the main plot is about a love triangle between a woman and two men from very different backgrounds. In *Pearl Harbor* (2001) the main plot is the love triangle between two fighter pilots and a beautiful woman. In *Troy* (2004) the main plot is the adulterous relationship between Paris and Helen, the wife of the king of Sparta.

Romcoms (romantic comedies) have had a very significant effect on the relationship culture because romantic relationships often play an important part in their storylines. Romcoms strongly promote the idea that relationships are a way of having fun rather than a way of finding a future spouse. However, romcoms do not explain the real dangers of relationships.

Four Weddings and a Funeral (1994) is a British romcom about a group of friends who go through various romantic relationships. The film is one of the most financially successful British films, having received over £200 million in revenue. The film is about how certain people 'fancy' other people, even when those people are married to others. Another famous and popular romcom is *American Pie* (1999). *American Pie* promotes the idea that all teenagers should be experimenting with sex and that the experimentation can be fun. The message of the above films is that you can play around with sex without any emotional or physical damage.

One of the most famous romcoms is *Love Actually* (2003). This 15-rated film is promoted as family entertainment and is so popular that it is often shown at Christmas time in the UK. The film is about ten romantic relationships that develop in the weeks leading up to Christmas Day. There are various humorous aspects about the way the relationships develop. Sadly, the film glamorizes promiscuity, lust, adultery and filthy language. The film clearly has a message that lust and sex outside of marriage are morally fine. It also sends a message that it is fine to get divorced if you want to change your partner.

Some recent films have even gone so far as to say that casual sex is fine. The romcom *Friends with Benefits* (2011) is based around the idea that if your 'friend' gives you sexual favours, this will be a kind of special benefit from that friend.

Recent films such as *The Karate Kid* (2010) and *Moonrise Kingdom* (2012) show children as young as twelve having an intimate kiss. As a result of the film industry people now assume that it is normal to have intimate relationships from a young age, despite the fact that this is far away from the age when people can marry.

Even though Hollywood films glamorize sex and lust outside of marriage, they rarely show the harmful consequences of such behaviour. They do not show the full trauma of relationship break-ups and they do not show the misery of a lifetime of failed relationships. The entertainment industry also does not show that saving yourself for marriage is good for individuals and society.

2. Television and the relationship culture

Since television became popular in the 1950s there has been a steady increase in the promotion of sex outside of marriage. Secular studies by the University of Michigan published in 2010 showed the following statistics for television programmes watched by teenagers in the USA:

- 70 per cent of the top twenty most-watched shows by teenagers include sexual content.

- From 1998 to 2010 the number of sex scenes on TV has nearly doubled.

- 15 per cent of scenes with sexual intercourse involve characters who have just met.

- Of the shows with sexual content, there is an average of five sexual scenes per hour.

- Watching sex on TV increases the chances a teenager will have sexual relationships.

- There is very little content about the dangers of sexual activity.[2]

Since teenagers watch an average of around three hours of TV per day, that corresponds to seeing around ten scenes with some kind of sexual content each day. That equates to 3,650 scenes with sexual content per year, and over 18,000 sexual scenes from the age of thirteen to the age of eighteen. Of those scenes, the majority involve sexual activity outside of marriage and a significant proportion involve people who have just met. Even though the study was confined to the USA, the figures are typical of television throughout Western society. The daily message given by television is that sex outside of marriage is normal and safe.

The University of Michigan also found that most parents do not speak to their children about sex. This means that teenagers rely on television to get their moral standards. Since the entertainment industry is saturating teenagers' minds with immoral sexual content it should be no wonder that there is a relentless rise in sexual immorality in Western society.

Sitcoms and the relationship culture

The following key milestones in the history of British situation comedies illustrate the decline of moral standards over the last fifty years:

MILESTONES OF SEXUAL CONTENT

1965–1975 *Till Death Us Do Part* (BBC 1)—sexual jokes.

1973 *Casanova* (BBC 1)—sexual innuendos.

1979–1981 *Agony* (ITV)—gay character not object of ridicule.

1989–1998 *Birds of a Feather* (BBC 1)—Dorien Green seeking extramarital sex.

1991–1995 *Bottom* (BBC 2)—crude, immoral sexual jokes.

2008–2010 *The Inbetweeners* (E4)—immoral sexual references and jokes.[3]

Situation comedies are assumed to be just entertainment and fun. However, they have had a detrimental effect on the moral standards of society. Sitcoms often portray marriage as boring and relationships as exciting, and these stereotypes have a big influence on viewers. When someone laughs at jokes about lust and adultery, he or she can become accepting of that behaviour and blind to the consequences. As with films, sitcoms do not explain the real dangers of intimate relationships.

Soap operas and the relationship culture

In the early days of television there were wholesome drama series such as *The Waltons* and *Little House on the Prairie* which generally promoted marriage and biblical standards of courtship. However, in order to make money, television series were quick to adopt the relationship culture. Soap operas such as *Friends, Neighbours, Emmerdale, Coronation Street* and *EastEnders* give the message that serial relationships and sex before marriage are normal behaviour and that it can be a source of pleasure to gossip about other people's relationships.

Soap operas have such a powerful effect on the behaviour of society that they are now given social impact awards for the way they raise social awareness of issues such as reporting of rape. But while there may be some positive social impact, soaps have a very negative impact in the way they promote sexual immorality. Soaps contain immoral behaviour that is designed to entertain the audience and get higher ratings. There is inevitably a vicious circle in that the moral standards of soaps are designed to be lower than those of society and the moral standards of society are dragged down by the standards of soaps—and so the declining cycle goes on.

The Rand Corporation in the USA researched the effect of popular teenage programmes, including *Friends*, on teenage behaviour and published their findings in the *Journal of Pediatrics* in 2008. *Friends* was judged to be a sexually charged programme with high sexual dialogue. Teenage pregnancies were found to be twice as common among those who watched programmes like *Friends* compared with those who did not.

3. Pop music and the relationship culture

Pop music has had a very significant effect on the rise of sexual immorality. Since the 1960s one of the main themes of pop music has been getting sexual pleasure in relationships. Many pop songs have phrases such as 'I want your body' and 'let's get physical'. A harmful feature of modern pop music is accompanying videos which show sexual dancing and seductive dress.

In recent times some popular singers like Rihanna have chosen to simulate sexual acts in their dance routines. Such videos at present do not have an adult rating, although this is being considered. When most young people spend a large proportion of time listening to and watching such pop videos, it is no wonder they are experimenting with relationships and sex from a young age.

Many pop songs describe the negative emotions involved in a relationship break-up, such as anger, regret, sadness and devastation. The songs show clearly that a relationship split is a type of divorce. It is interesting to note that many pop stars live broken lives with many relationship break-ups and so their songs are speaking from real experience. It is ironic that pop stars try to give comfort through pop songs to people who are recovering from relationship break-ups, because it is pop singers and pop songs that have encouraged people to have relationships in the first place!

Another message of pop music is that young people do not need to involve their parents in courtship. If you analyse a thousand pop songs, while the majority encourage sexual intimacy, there may not be a single song that encourages a person to honour his or her parents. When young people are constantly listening to such music, it is not surprising that they do not think to speak to their parents about courtship.

4. Radio and the relationship culture

Some of the popular radio channels in the UK, such as Radio 1, play a big part in promoting the relationship culture. Not only do they play pop songs that encourage relationships, but also the presenters often talk about relationships and sexual attraction. On Radio 1 it is common for presenters to discuss charts of celebrities who are ranked in terms of how sexually attractive they are. Such discussions promote lust and seductive behaviour as morally fine. Radio 1 has a large audience, with many people starting to listen in their teenage years, so it has a powerful influence on society.

One recent trend in modern media is the use of sexual innuendos (subtle sexual humour). One of the most widely broadcast adverts on the radio in the UK between 2008 and 2012 was the BT advert for Maureen, which is a name given to the BT Directory of Enquiries. This advert joked about Maureen as if she was a prostitute. She was described as one 'who gives you more' and 'is cheap'. This advert has been heard by millions of people in the UK, including millions of children. The message to children is that a key goal in life is to get sexual pleasures from relationships, and that some people are more willing than others to provide those sexual pleasures.

5. Pornography and the relationship culture

Pornography is a significant part of the entertainment industry and generates many billions of dollars in revenue every year. Over the last hundred years there has been a gradual acceptance of pornography as a morally acceptable form of entertainment. Most hotels now offer pornography in their rooms and pornography is widely available on the Internet. This should not be surprising because when society rejects the teaching of Jesus on lust it is inevitable that almost every kind of lust-based activity is seen as acceptable.

When D. H. Lawrence wrote his explicit novel *Lady Chatterley's Lover* in 1928 he could not get it published in the UK because society considered it immoral and publishers would have been prosecuted for obscenity. However in 1960 *Lady Chatterley's Lover* was published unabridged by Penguin following a trial for obscenity that was defeated. The *Fifty Shades* erotic novel trilogy, published from 2011 to 2012, shows how pornography has now become acceptable in society as mainstream entertainment. The novels quickly became bestsellers and the film version of *Fifty Shades of Grey* has generated $500 million in sales.

There is an important connection between pornography and the relationship culture. Much pornography promotes the idea that casual sex outside of marriage is fine and that people should seek to have sex for pleasure. When society accepts pornography as morally fine it is inevitable that there will be a relationship culture in which people seek sexual pleasures outside of marriage.

6. Media coverage of celebrity relationships

Many newspapers and TV channels give a significant amount of coverage to news of celebrity relationships, thus giving the message that relationships are important. Even though the media may criticize celebrities for certain excesses, there is rarely criticism of their immoral relationships and lifestyles. Since relationships make the most sensational news, people are constantly bombarded with the relationship culture and they inevitably copy that culture. Sadly, there are many young children who aspire to have relationships from a young age in order to emulate their celebrity idols.

When Prince William was living with Kate Middleton before they were married, this was considered by the media to be morally fine because they were 'in a relationship'. In reality they were living in sin and setting an example that was doing damage to the institution of marriage. As a result of the widespread media coverage of William and Kate living together before marriage, many young people will now consider it morally fine to live together outside of marriage.

7. Distorted television adaptations of classic novels

Some modern TV adaptations of period novels have been seriously distorted and 'sexed up' to gain higher ratings. For example, in 2007 ITV broadcast a series of three adaptations of Jane Austen's novels *Mansfield Park*, *Northanger Abbey* and *Persuasion* which were 'sexed up' by giving actresses revealing clothing such as plunging necklines and by making the actors behave in a flirtatious way. Such adaptations also show couples engaging in sexual acts such as intimate kissing before engagement.

It is sad how such misleading adaptations lead viewers to think that people behaved in a sexually permissive way in past ages when this was not the case. Instead of period novels being an important testimony to a biblical way of courtship, they are now being used to reinforce the immoral teaching that it is fine to lust and have sex outside of marriage.

8. Comparing the lifestyles of actors with their screen roles

It can be quite instructive to compare the actual lifestyles of actors and actresses with the roles they play on-screen to show how standards have declined in modern times. Many of the actors who act out roles involving purity before marriage actually live immoral lifestyles themselves. Whereas one of the leading actors in the 2007 BBC1 adaptation of *Cranford* (Simon Woods, who plays Dr Harrison) follows the biblical courtship process with great innocence, he has a homosexual lifestyle in real life.

In the 2014 BBC1 adaptation of *Little Dorrit* by Charles Dickens one of the lead parts is a man called Arthur Clennam, who behaves in an extremely patient and pure way towards young women. When he proposes to Pet Meagles there has not been even a single intimate kiss, and when he eventually proposes to Amy they have had no relationship or physical intimacy. Yet in real life the actor who plays Mr Clennam (Matthew Macfadyen) was responsible for taking another man's wife (Keeley Hawes) when she had been married for just eleven weeks.

9. How Western governments have failed to provide a moral lead

As the moral standards of films declined during the twentieth century church leaders and public pressure groups called for action. In 1930 public pressure led to a censorship code in the USA called the Hays Code, which tried to ban immoral behaviour in films. But this code had limited success in influencing a powerful film industry.

In the UK in 1965 Mary Whitehouse started the National Viewers' and Listeners' Association (NVLA) with the aim of cleaning up television. But this had limited success, with television producers largely ignoring the call to promote good moral standards. Today the NVLA has changed its name to Mediawatch-UK and is still calling for better moral standards in film and television but is having limited success.

Sadly, Western governments have done little over the last hundred years to stop the moral decline in entertainment. In recent times governments have established guidelines to protect children, such as the watershed, which limits sexual content before a certain time; but such guidelines have done little to stop the general moral decline in film and television.

One of the reasons why governments do little is because they are fearful of the media. Whereas the entertainment industry is driven by money, politicians are driven mainly by popularity. And a way to be popular is not to fight against the media and the entertainment industry.

One example of politicians bowing to the media is the legalization of gay marriage and gay adoption. In 2003 David Cameron and many Conservatives in the UK voted against the repeal of Section 28 because they did not approve of homosexuality being promoted in schools in the UK. However, in recent years the same Conservatives have voted for gay marriage and the promotion of homosexuality, knowing that they would be criticized by the popular media if they did not conform to the media's view of moral standards.

10. How state education has failed to provide a moral lead

In the first half of the twentieth century children were taught that there should be abstinence before marriage. There was no need for 'sex education' because children were not sexually active and were not expected to be sexually active. As many young people became sexually active in the mid-twentieth century due to the influence of the entertainment industry the government introduced 'sex education'. From the 1970s the focus of sex education has been to promote safe sex without any moral framework. By not giving any moral framework, there has been an implied message that it is fine to have sex outside of marriage.

The change from 'sex education' to 'sex and relationships education' (SRE) in 1999 is very significant. A hundred years ago it would have been assumed that 'sex and marriage' went together, and if there was any sex education it would have been called 'sex and marriage education' (SME). But now it is assumed that 'sex and relationships' go together, and so the state is teaching that sex outside of marriage is morally fine.

In 1987 the Sex Education Forum (SEF) was established as the national authority on sex and relationships education in the UK. The SEF believes that children should be taught that there are no moral absolutes in sexual behaviour. In 2013 SEF started publishing a magazine called the *Sex Educational Supplement* to give schools advice and guidance on sex education. In the first issue in 2013 the magazine focused on pornography and stated that pornography is not necessarily wrong. The SEF is an example of how the modern education system ignores biblical teaching and copies the moral standards of the entertainment industry.

Even though sex education is intended to reduce unwanted pregnancies and sexual diseases, it fails to recognize that the only solution is to go back to biblical standards of courtship and abstinence. What sex education should do is teach that abstinence is morally right and has the advantage of avoiding the problems of the relationship culture. Sadly, that teaching is not given. In the USA there are organizations that promote abstinence before marriage, but these are generally not allowed into state schools. Many Christian parents ask for their children to be withdrawn from sex education classes in state schools because they recognize the inherent immoral message of the sex education.

The drop in moral standards can be clearly seen in the provision of university accommodation. Prior to 1960, male and female students were generally put into separate halls and strict rules were applied to prevent male students going near female rooms. However, male and female students are now located close together with few rules on segregation. As a consequence, university halls are often a place of promiscuous sexual activity. In addition, there has been a very significant rise in sexual assaults on women in universities and colleges.

11. The relationship culture and the church

At the time of the sexual revolution of the 1960s most Christians did not copy the world but continued to follow biblical standards of courtship. Christians could see that the relationship culture was anti-biblical and an invention of a modern society that had rebelled against biblical standards.

However, the relationship culture has gradually entered the church. Most teenage Christians watch many hours of the world's entertainment every week and get the message that it is normal to have relationships from a young age. When those Christians go to church it is often the case that there is not much teaching on biblical standards of courtship and the dangers of the relationship culture.

In addition, some recent Christian authors have claimed that it is fine to have a degree of sexual intimacy outside of marriage. As a consequence, many young Christians are following the relationship culture and living an ungodly lifestyle.

Young Christians are often under great pressure from friends to have relationships, and sometimes that peer pressure even comes from within the church. The question 'Have you had your first boyfriend/girlfriend yet?' implies that people should have a boyfriend or girlfriend for the sake of it. When a girl is being told by her friends that what she needs is a boyfriend, this puts great pressure on her to conform to the relationship culture.

Many Christian leaders now see the importance of promoting biblical standards in courtship and there are signs of reformation in this area. Christian authors such as Joshua Harris, the late Elisabeth Elliot, Heather Paulsen, Sarah Mally and Joel James have called for Christians to return to biblical standards of courtship, and many Christians have responded to that call.

Notes

1 From Filmsite, http://www.filmsite.org (accessed June 2015).
2 'Television and Children', University of Michigan Health System, August 2010, http://www.med.umich.edu/yourchild/topics/tv.htm.
3 From Filmsite.

BIBLICAL TEACHING
ON MARRIAGE SHOWS
WHY IT IS BEST NOT
TO USE THE TERM
'RELATIONSHIP' TO
DESCRIBE A ROMANTIC
FRIENDSHIP.

2. God's way: stay pure before marriage

Key biblical principle: BEING JOINED TOGETHER IS FOR MARRIAGE ONLY (GEN. 2:24)

Genesis 2:24 contains foundational teaching on romance and marriage: 'Therefore a man shall leave his father and mother and be joined to his wife, and they shall become one flesh.' The clear implication of this verse is that marriage is the only place where a man and woman can be joined together and belong to each other. Genesis 2:24 does not say that a man shall leave his mother and father and be joined to a series of partners with the option of eventually being joined to a wife. The teaching of this verse is so important that it was repeated by the Lord Jesus in Matthew 19:6 and by the apostle Paul in Ephesians 5:31. Matthew 19:6 also explains that it is God who joins two people together in a marriage relationship.

One reason why I like watching period dramas on television is because they reveal the beauty and safety of biblical standards of courtship. In the nineteenth-century novel *Cranford* by Elizabeth Gaskell, Major Gordon and Jessie are very attracted to each other for several years before they are in a position to get engaged because of family and work duties. Despite being really attracted to each other for so long, they avoid becoming a couple and have no physical intimacy. Only when they get engaged do they see themselves as a couple and tell others they are together. Their restraint makes their eventual marriage very special. In contrast, there is great peer pressure in modern society for an unmarried person to have sexual relationships in which he or she belongs to someone else.

This chapter gives nine biblical reasons why it is right to stay pure before marriage.

1. Marriage is the only place to belong to someone romantically

Therefore a man shall leave his father and mother and be joined to his wife, and they shall become one flesh (Gen. 2:24).

As mentioned at the start of the chapter, this verse teaches that marriage is the only place where a man and a woman can become one and give their hearts and their bodies to each other. Since oneness (and sexual intimacy) is for marriage, courtship should not involve being joined together as a formal couple but should be a friendship where the goal is to explore the possibility of a future marriage relationship.

The title of Brian and Barbara Edwards' book on marriage, *No Longer Two*,[1] illustrates the vital biblical truth that two people should only become one in marriage. A key problem with the modern relationship culture is that it makes people believe they can become one outside of marriage and have sexual intimacy outside of marriage.

The Christian marriage ceremony emphasizes that marriage is the only place where two people can belong to each other. The traditional marriage ceremony has phrases such as 'with my body I thee worship', 'to love and to cherish' and 'to have and to hold from this day forward'. Such marriage vows would not make sense if it was morally fine for people to give away their hearts and bodies before marriage.

The fact that marriage should be lifelong is highlighted in Malachi 2:14, which states that a man has a wife by covenant. Only death should separate a man and a woman who have given their hearts and bodies to each other. When people follow the biblical model of romance they will have either just one partner in life or perhaps more than one partner if their spouse dies and they remarry. In contrast, the relationship culture leads to people having several or many sexual partners in life.

Biblical teaching on marriage shows why it is best not to use the term 'relationship' to describe a romantic friendship. When two people say they are 'in a relationship', the phrase means that the two people are joined together and have, to some extent, given their hearts and bodies to each other. Dictionaries generally define a romantic relationship as a relationship with sexual intimacy and the joining together of two people.

Again, in the traditional marriage service, the church minister sometimes says that the two people have 'chosen a love' and now they must spend the rest of their lives 'loving their choice'. This helpful statement emphasizes that courtship should be a means to an end (to choose a love) and not an end in itself (to love a choice). The problem with the term 'relationship' is that it implies that two people have made their choice and are now loving their choice. Avoiding the terminology of the relationship culture can help Christians send a message to others that they are staying pure before marriage.

There are several ways of describing a romantic friendship in a Bible-honouring way. You can say you are 'going out' with someone, 'courting' someone or 'dating' someone. Although it is now considered old-fashioned, I think the best term is 'courting' because it means *courting the possibility* of being joined together in a marriage relationship. Courtship emphasizes that a person is making a choice, not loving a choice.

2. Marriage and romance are sacred

Modern society believes that people can have relationships as an alternative to marriage. But it is dishonouring to marriage to make an alternative man-made relationship culture. There are several biblical reasons why marriage is sacred:

- Marriage is blessed by God (Gen. 1:27–28).
- Marriage was instituted at the beginning of creation (Gen. 2:24).
- Marriage was instituted before the Fall of man (Gen. 2:24).
- Marriage involves God joining two people together (Matt. 19:6).
- Marriage is a picture of Christ and the church (Eph. 5:25).
- Marriage was a picture of God's relationship to Israel (Ezek. 16:8).
- Marriage involves a lifelong covenant (Mal. 2:14).
- Marriage is to be honoured by all (Heb. 13:4).

These verses make it very clear that marriage is sacred and very special in God's sight. One meaning of sacred is 'too important to be changed or interfered with'. One of the most important ways for a society to keep marriage sacred is not to have a relationship culture. The relationship culture devalues marriage because relationships are an alternative to marriage.

The sacredness of marriage can be illustrated by considering how relationships are not sacred. Relationships are not blessed by God; relationships were not instituted at creation; relationships do not involve two people being joined by God; relationships are not a picture of Christ and the church; relationships do not involve a lifelong covenant; and the Bible nowhere says that relationships are honourable.

Marriage is sacred because sex and romance are sacred. Relationships are dishonouring to marriage because they cheapen sex and romance as something to play around with from a young age. Relationships are dishonouring because they do not have any binding agreement. The very term 'relationship' illustrates the cheapness of the relationship culture. People have relationships with their neighbours, their work colleagues and even their pets. To say that having a romantic 'relationship' gives permission to have sexual intimacy is very dishonouring to marriage.

Classic novels show how in past societies it was considered unbiblical if people had relationships outside of marriage. In Charles Dickens's novel *Little Dorrit* a man called Mr Gowan has an illicit relationship with a woman called Miss Wade when they are both young and single, and that is considered to be immoral. Jane Austen has characters in her novels who have illicit relationships, such as Mr Willoughby in *Sense and Sensibility* and Mr Wickham in *Pride and Prejudice*.

Of course, past societies that practised courtship were far from perfect and there was always a proportion of people in every community who did not follow the courtship process. However, there was peer pressure for people to respect marriage and save themselves for marriage.

3. Divorce and separation are traumatic and contrary to God's design

> For the LORD God of Israel says
> That He hates divorce,
> For it covers one's garment with violence
> (Mal. 2:16).

Modern society believes that relationship splits are necessary and to be expected, but the Bible teaches that God hates divorce and separation. The Bible teaches that divorce is contrary to God's design and to be avoided as much as possible. Divorce is justified only in extreme cases such as sexual immorality (Matt. 19:9), abuse or the departure of an unbeliever. Relationship splits are a type of divorce and therefore should not be condoned or seen as necessary.

Of course, if someone has only one relationship and that leads to marriage, that person will not have gone through a divorce-like split. However, the overwhelming expectation of the relationship culture is that people will have many relationships before they get married (if they marry at all), and will therefore experience many relationship splits.

Relationship splits are a type of divorce because they involve the separation of two people who were joined together. When people say 'we are separating' or 'we have split', they are admitting that they are undergoing a type of divorce. As with divorce, relationship splits are often very traumatic. Before the split takes place there are powerful emotional ties, pledges of love, physical intimacy and dreams of a future together. As soon as there is a split, the dreams are shattered and there is the tearing apart of the relationship.

When relationships end, people often feel regret that they have given their bodies and affections to those from whom they are now effectively divorced. The splitting-up of a relationship is not necessarily as serious as a marital divorce, but it is still a type of divorce and therefore something that God hates.

Biblical courtship honours the teaching of Scripture on divorce because, if courtship ends without an accepted proposal of marriage, there is not a relationship split. In period dramas it is noticeable that people never have relationship splits and there is no talk of ex-boyfriends and ex-girlfriends. Of course, it can be very disappointing if courtship ends without engagement. However, there is no divorce-like separation.

Some people argue that relationships can have value even if they end in a relationship split. But how can a relationship have value when it ends in the failure of separation? Failure, by definition, cannot be valuable. Every time people have relationship splits, they are experiencing the failure of divorce. They are also increasing the chances of their future marriage ending in divorce because they are getting used to the practice of separating from their partner when things are not going well.

Some have also tried to argue that relationship splits themselves can be considered a positive experience. In recent years some have used the term 'conscious uncoupling' to describe the separation of two people who were in a relationship. The idea is that two people can consciously decide to uncouple themselves in a completely positive way. However, the Bible teaches that the ending of a romantic relationship is always a traumatic event.

4. The Bible recognizes only the single, engaged and married statuses

Modern society says that people can be single, married or 'in a relationship'. However, the relationship status is not found in the Bible. The Bible gives clear approval of marriage (Gen. 2:24), engagement (Matt. 1:18) and the single status (1 Cor. 7:32), but there is no approval of the relationship status or couple status.

The Bible gives guidance on every aspect of human living and moral conduct, especially in the book of Proverbs and the New Testament. Relationships have such a major impact on people's lives that the Bible would certainly give approval for relationships if they were morally acceptable. It is not possible to argue that God approves of relationships but has simply not given any approval or guidance on them in the Bible. In fact, there are strong biblical arguments why the relationship status is unbiblical.

In 1 Corinthians 7:32–33 the apostle Paul clearly implies that all adults are either married or unmarried and there is therefore no 'relationship' category. In 1 Corinthians 7:32 Paul says, 'But I want you to be without care. He who is unmarried cares for the things of the Lord—how he may please the Lord.' There is a key assumption in this verse that *anyone* who is unmarried should be free to serve the Lord. In order for a single person to be free to serve the Lord, he or she cannot be in a marriage-like relationship. Paul does not say, 'He who is unmarried, or not in a relationship, cares for the things of the Lord.'

The book of Proverbs has many verses relating to marriage and the roles of husbands and wives. However, there is no approval of the relationship status to be found in the book. Proverbs says, 'He who finds a wife finds a good thing' (Prov. 18:22)—not 'He who finds a wife or girlfriend/relationship finds a good thing'. Proverbs further says that 'a prudent wife is from the Lord' (Prov. 19:14)—not that 'a prudent wife or girlfriend is from the Lord'. These verses also emphasize that courtship is about *finding* a partner, not *having* a partner. Proverbs has many verses describing sexual immorality as a serious sin, especially in chapters 5–7. These verses are directly applicable to relationships outside of marriage.

Some may argue that there is little mention of biblical courtship in the Bible. However, the whole point of courtship is that it is just a friendship, not an official relationship, so we would not expect to see details of courtship in the Bible. Others may argue that arranged marriages were common in biblical times. However, this does not change the fact that people avoided relationships in Bible times.

In biblical narrative accounts of people's lives there is no mention of single people being attached in romantic relationships before engagement other than in sinful situations. An example of a relationship being explicitly labelled as sinful is that of the woman at the well, who was in a relationship with a man who was not her husband (John 4:7–26). Another example of a relationship being sinful is that of Samson and Delilah (Judg. 16:4).

5. The Bible commands people not to awaken love until marriage

Do not stir up nor awaken love
Until it pleases
(S. of S. 2:7).

Modern society says that love can be awakened in casual relationships from a young age. But the Bible commands us three times not to awaken love before its proper time (S. of S. 2:7; 3:5; 8:4). In his Bible commentary,[2] John MacArthur explains that these verses refer to the commitment of the Shulamite woman to a chaste life not just during marriage but also *before* marriage. Living a chaste life involves keeping sexual purity before the wedding night. The fact that the command is given three times emphasizes the importance of purity before marriage.

Even though the book of the Song of Solomon contains much symbolism of the marriage between Christ and the church, the teaching is also applicable to courtship and marriage. The verses cited above show that romantic love is something that a person has a responsibility to control and save for marriage. In the same way that a married person should not love someone other than his or her spouse, so a single person should not allow him- or herself to be joined in a relationship before marriage.

Rowina Seidler, who has written articles on biblical standards of courtship, says, 'It is not loving to stir up another's love outside of commitment. It is not loving to treat someone as if they are yours when you have not committed to keeping them.'[3]

6. The Bible commands people to love as Christ loved the church

> ... that He might present her to Himself a glorious church, not having spot or wrinkle or any such thing, but that she should be holy and without blemish (Eph. 5:27).

Modern society says that people should not aim to stay pure before marriage, but the Bible clearly teaches that sexual purity before marriage is important. The picture of Christ and the church is relevant to courtship because husbands are commanded to love their wives 'as Christ also loved the church' (Eph. 5:25). The church is a bride who will be without spot or wrinkle when presented to Christ (5:27).

One way the church is to keep herself pure is by not loving the world. In contrast, Israel was called an unfaithful bride-to-be for having a relationship with the world (Hosea 9:1). One of the reasons why the marriage between Christ and the church is so beautiful is because Christ is pure and the church will be pure. It follows that people should aim to keep themselves pure before marriage so that they can give that gift of purity (or a period of purity) to their future spouse.

A bride is right to go to great lengths to make herself physically beautiful on her wedding day. But the beauty of saving your heart and body for your spouse is much more important than physical beauty. Purity is priceless and far more desirable than beautiful clothing and make-up. If you ask a man whether he would prefer a low-key wedding with a bride who was a virgin or a very glamorous wedding with a bride who was not a virgin, he would almost certainly ask for the low-key wedding with a virgin bride. Likewise, a woman would almost certainly prefer a bridegroom who had kept himself pure for his bride.

7. The Bible commands people to save their love for their spouse

> Remove your way far from her [an immoral woman],
> And do not go near the door of her house,
> Lest you give your honor to others,
> And your years to the cruel one ...
> Drink water from your own cistern,
> And running water from your own well ...
> And rejoice with the wife of your youth
> (Prov. 5:8–9, 15, 18).

Modern society says that people should not worry about the feelings of a future spouse, but the Bible teaches that people should save themselves for marriage. Proverbs exhorts a husband to rejoice in the wife of his youth and not to give his honour and time to others. Proverbs 5 is relevant regarding not just adultery but also relationships before marriage. A person should not have intimate relationships before marriage but should save his or her emotional energy for a future spouse.

People have their greatest beauty and strength in their younger years. It is sad if the greatest beauty and strength of a person are enjoyed by romantic 'partners' rather than by his or her spouse. It is common for non-Christians to get married after spending ten to twenty years having a series of relationships during which they give away their hearts and bodies. Those people have given their best youthful years to people other than their spouse.

The book of Proverbs explains that 'a companion of harlots' wastes his wealth (Prov. 29:3). This truth is illustrated in the story of the prodigal son, who wasted some of his youthful years on prostitutes (Luke 15:11–32), but the principle can also be seen widely today when people have relationships. Most young people are wasting much of their time, emotions and money on relationships that end in failure.

In her book *Emotional Purity*[4] Heather Paulsen emphasizes the importance of saving one's heart for one's future spouse. She recommends that during courtship a man and a woman constantly remember that they may not marry each other and therefore they should not get emotionally attached to each other. In so doing they are both honouring their future spouses.

Heather Paulsen uses the illustration of a Post-it note. If you reuse a Post-it note several times, it becomes less effective. In the same way, when people have many relationships, they are using up their emotional energy. When they eventually get married, they find they have already used up much of their emotional energy on other people.

8. The Bible commands people to do good to their spouse all their life

> Who can find a virtuous wife?
> For her worth is far above rubies.
> The heart of her husband safely trusts her;
> So he will have no lack of gain.
> She does him good and not evil
> All the days of her life
> (Prov. 31:10–12).

Modern society says that people should not worry about doing good to their spouse. But Proverbs 31:12 teaches that a virtuous wife does good to her husband all the days of her life. Of course, the main application is that a wife will be supportive throughout her marriage. However, notice the wording 'all the days of her life': this period of time actually includes the days before she was married. One application of this verse is that a virtuous wife will avoid having relationships before marriage so that she can save her heart for her future husband.

In *Emotional Purity* Heather Paulsen helpfully explains that the goal for a woman during courtship is not to be a good girlfriend but to be a good wife in the future by staying pure during courtship. Douglas Wilson wrote a book entitled *Fidelity: What It Means to Be a One-Woman Man*[5] because it is equally right for a man to save himself for his future wife.

9. The Bible commands us to honour our parents

Genesis 2:24 teaches that we are subject to our parents until marriage. Of course, when we are adults we have much more freedom and are subject to our parents in a largely symbolic sense. However, the clear implication of Genesis 2:24 is that marriage is the only family relationship that can legitimately supersede the parent–child relationship.

With biblical courtship there is no diminishing of the relationship with parents because there is no sense of belonging to someone else. Courtship also encourages people to consult their parents about whom they should court and marry, because they are still subject to their parents.

In contrast to biblical teaching, modern society says that people can become fully independent of their parents at the age of eighteen. Even before that age romantic relationships encourage people to diminish ties with their parents because they have created new ties with their 'partner'. The relationship culture often leads to people not involving their parents in the choice of a partner. When a person sees relationships simply as fun and not necessarily leading to marriage, it is not surprising if they do not seek parental advice about their relationships.

The diminished role of parents is bad for society because young people are making life-changing decisions without the safety check of parental advice. The Bible warns that problems will come to those who do not honour their parents. One of the reasons why we live in a troubled society is because children are rebelling against parents, and one of the reasons for that is the relationship culture.

Notes

1 **Brian and Barbara Edwards,** *No Longer Two: A Christian Guide for Engagement and Marriage* (rev. ed.; Leominster: Day One, 2009).

2 *The MacArthur Study Bible* (Nashville: Word Publishing, 1997).

3 **Rowina Seidler,** *Ruby in the Rough: Biblical Principles to Set Women Free,* http://www.rubyintherough.co.uk/.

4 **Heather Arnel Paulsen,** *Emotional Purity: An Affair of the Heart* (Wheaton, IL: Crossway).

5 **Douglas Wilson,** *Fidelity: What It Means to Be a One-Woman Man* (Moscow, ID: Canon Press, 1999).

WHEN CONSIDERING
GOING OUT WITH
SOMEONE IT IS
IMPORTANT TO THINK
ABOUT YOUR TRUE
MOTIVES ... THE ONLY
GODLY, SAFE AND
LOVING MOTIVE IS THAT
OF INVESTIGATING
MARRIAGE.

3. How to stay pure before marriage

Key biblical principle: BE CAUTIOUS IN CHOOSING A SPOUSE (PROV. 12:26)

The importance of choosing friends carefully is explained in Proverbs 12:26: 'The righteous should choose his friends carefully, for the way of the wicked leads them astray.' A spouse is generally the most important friend we will have in this world, so a Christian has a responsibility to do all he or she can to be careful about that choice. One of the most important ways to be careful in courtship is to court only in order to investigate marriage.

In the TV period drama series *Cranford* the young Doctor Harrison asks Miss Hutton's father for permission to court Miss Hutton. In the discussion with Miss Hutton's father, Doctor Harrison explains that his motivation is that he intends to propose marriage to Miss Hutton. Doctor Harrison states that his intentions are entirely honourable, which means that he is not going to use courtship as a means of gaining sexual pleasures or having the fun of a relationship.

This chapter describes different things you can do to save yourself for marriage.

1. Only start courting if you want to explore the possibility of marriage

When considering going out with someone it is important to think about your true motives. Do you really want to investigate marriage, or is your real motive to seek the pleasures of having a relationship? The only godly, safe and loving motive is that of investigating marriage.

The motive you have for courting has a huge influence on what type of person you choose to court. When exploring the possibility of marriage, a person will inevitably think very carefully about the character of the other person, knowing there are lifelong consequences to the choice. In contrast, if a person's motive is that of short-term pleasure, he or she will be tempted to make a choice based on superficial factors such as looks or fashion. But such superficial attractions can lead to a person slipping into a relationship that he or she regrets starting and finds hard to finish.

The motive you have for courting can also affect your behaviour during courtship. If your motive is to explore marriage, you will focus on learning about the other person rather than seeking sexual pleasures. If you are courting for pleasure, it is tempting to seek higher levels of pleasure over time and push the boundaries of sexual intimacy.

Another reason to court only when there is interest in marriage is that it can be very misleading to the other person to enter into courtship if you are not focused on marriage. It is disrespectful and unloving to make someone think you are interested in marriage when you actually have little interest in marriage. I know of a Christian man who was shocked when his Christian girlfriend confessed one day that she would never be prepared to marry him, despite being happy to be his girlfriend! He felt misled and was sad that he had wasted a lot of time and emotion.

Since the goal of courtship is to consider marriage, the man should be sensitive to the fact that he will have to decide whether and when to make a proposal of marriage, and the woman should be sensitive to the fact that she will have to decide whether she would accept a proposal of marriage. This does not mean that courtship should involve a preoccupation with marriage proposals, but it does mean that the two people should not forget the ultimate aim of courtship.

In general, the man should take the lead in developing the friendship and should make the proposal of marriage (if there is a proposal). This is because the Bible teaches that the husband is the head in marriage (Eph. 5:23) and it is the man who should find a wife (Prov. 18:22). The man should take the responsibility to make sure that the friendship is pure and unpressurized.

With today's twenty-four-hour communications it is important to be careful not to make excessive contact. Sending fifty texts a day may be tempting for a young man who is very keen on a young lady he has just met, but such intense contact does not follow the principle of choosing friends carefully.

Since courtship should have the main goal of investigating marriage, it follows that when they start courting a couple should be old enough, or approaching an age when they will be old enough, to marry. In the UK this means that before starting to court they should be at least sixteen *and* in a position to marry in the not-too-distant future. They should also have the maturity for marriage before starting to court.

Some people worry that by avoiding relationships they will not make progress in finding a spouse, but the opposite is true. By avoiding casual relationships that do not go anywhere, a person can focus on finding the right spouse. The fact that a godly Christian chooses not to follow the relationship culture does not mean that he or she takes little interest in the opposite sex. A godly Christian man can put great effort into finding a wife, and a godly woman can pray earnestly for a husband.

2. Do not be an official couple with marriage-like obligations
When courting there is a sense in which two people are a 'courting couple'. However, it is important not to be seen as a couple who belong to each other in a marriage-like relationship. A courting couple should be seen as being in a friendship rather than in a formal relationship. So when you start courting it is best to make your courtship low-key rather than broadcasting that you have become a courting couple. And it is best not to make your friendship too exclusive so that it appears that you belong to each other, especially in the early stages.

In the booklet *Help! I'm Confused about Dating*,[1] Joel James helpfully explains the biblical principle that courtship should be an unpressured friendship without marriage-like obligations such as belonging to each other.

By being in a friendship, two people can focus on making a prayerful and thoughtful choice about marriage rather than being preoccupied with meeting each other's emotional needs. Having a friendship also makes it easier to back out of courtship if you realize that you do not wish to marry the other person.

Keeping courtship low-key avoids the embarrassment that can be felt if the courtship ends without engagement. It also helps make engagement special if a proposal of marriage is accepted. One of the joys of engagement is that it is the point at which two people start to be seen as a couple. If you already look like a couple before engagement, you take away some of the joy of getting engaged.

Some people have such a low-key courtship that other people are very surprised when an engagement is announced. I remember attending a church when there was the exciting announcement of the engagement of two young people who had attended the church from their youth. The news was a complete surprise to almost the entire church (except the parents) because the two people had chosen to court in virtual secrecy! This is such a contrast with the relationship culture, in which romance is conducted in a very public way.

A key benefit of not being an official couple is that this helps to avoid other people monitoring and discussing the development of your romantic friendship. By not making a public declaration of being a couple you are giving the message to those around that the courtship is not for public scrutiny. One of the problems of relationships is that, because they are made public, other people are invited to take a public interest in them. When a relationship becomes official, other people feel they have a right to discuss that relationship in a public way. In the same way that people gossip about celebrity relationships, so people gossip about the relationships of their friends and work colleagues.

Interestingly, the modern relationship culture does sometimes have a brief phase when two people agree to be just friends in a type of courtship while they decide whether to start a relationship. When this happens the friendship period is often quite short, lasting typically just a few days or weeks. For Christians, the friendship phase should last for the whole of courtship until the point of engagement.

The start of courtship raises the question of whether a man should ask the woman's father for permission to start courting. This very much depends on the circumstances, such as the age of the people concerned and the local culture. A man must therefore be sensitive to the circumstances and act accordingly. If a woman is a teenager and living at home, it would usually be appropriate to speak to her father before starting to court her. In contrast, if a woman has left home, it may well not be necessary to speak to her father.

3. Do not have official start dates or anniversaries

With the relationship culture people are expected to officially announce the start of their relationship. However, the start of courtship is not something to make an official announcement about because it is simply the start of a process of making a decision about marriage. Engagement is the right time to make a formal announcement about becoming a couple because this is the point at which two people begin to formalize their commitment to each other and there is something that has been achieved.

When family and friends know that two people are going out with each other, they should be careful to be discreet about the courtship. That does not necessarily mean keeping the friendship a secret, but it does mean being careful not to give regular broadcasts about the details of the friendship. Romance is a delicate thing and should not receive a running public commentary.

It is also advisable not to have anniversaries of your courtship. When a married couple celebrate their first wedding anniversary, it is very precious and not something to copy. Because courtship is not an end in itself, there should be no reason to think in terms of achieving anniversaries. If courtship does not lead to engagement and marriage, there is no point in celebrating the first-year anniversary of that courtship. Because courtship generally involves the gradual development of a friendship, it is often not even possible to pinpoint the date of the beginning of the courtship.

4. Do not have relationship splits

If courtship comes to an end, it is important not to have a public announcement of a relationship split because this gives the impression that there has been a marriage-like relationship. When two people stop courting, they are simply stopping a process of courting the possibility of marriage.

In contrast, when people finish a relationship there is a public announcement and it is often a significant piece of news in the community. When people have a romantic relationship that keeps ending and starting again, it is sometimes referred to as an 'on-off' relationship. In contrast, people who are saving themselves for marriage cannot have an on-off relationship because they do not have a relationship in the first place.

People who court can finish the courtship at any time without having a relationship split and without feelings of guilt. As Sarah Mally and Joshua Harris have explained in their books,[2] with biblical standards of courtship there is always a positive outcome. If there is an accepted proposal of marriage, that is a very positive and happy outcome. On the other hand, if the courtship ends with no accepted proposal, this is still positive because there has been no loss of purity and no relationship split. Of course it can be very disappointing if there is no engagement, but each person can be thankful to the other for the friendship and for not violating his or her purity.

It is best not to use the phrases 'ex-boyfriend' or 'ex-girlfriend' because these give the impression that there was previously a relationship and there has been a type of divorce. If a Christian man is courting a Christian woman and the courtship comes to an end, other people can remark that the man had been 'keen' on the woman or had been 'sweet' on her, rather than talking in terms of 'ex-boyfriend' and 'ex-girlfriend'. When Christians are married it is best if they avoid saying to their spouses that someone they previously courted is their 'ex'.

5. Be cautious about making pledges of love

Since courtship involves a friendship, people who court should be very cautious about making pledges of love. The words 'I love you' imply a committed love, so it is best to use them only when you are sure you want to marry the other person. It can take many months to really get to know someone well enough to be able to decide whether you want to marry him or her. It takes time to know a person's character, beliefs and ambitions. Even though first impressions can be important, they can also be misleading. So it can take a long time before it is appropriate to say 'I love you'. One of the problems with the relationship culture is that people are very quick to give pledges of love, and this devalues the pledge of love.

6. Do not use the language of marriage

The terms 'husband', 'wife', 'joined', 'one flesh' and 'marriage' are precious terms that come directly from the Bible (Gen. 2:24; Matt. 19:5; Heb. 13:4). In order to honour marriage, these (or equivalent) terms should not be used outside of marriage. The relationship culture dishonours marriage by copying the language of marriage. The way society uses the term 'relationship' is dishonouring to marriage because it is an alternative to marriage. When two people start having a relationship, it is often said that they have 'become an item'. However, the expression 'we are an item' is dishonouring to marriage because it is a copy of the expression 'one flesh'.

When people start a relationship they will often say they now 'have a partner'. However, the term 'partner' is dishonouring to marriage because it is a replacement of the terms 'husband', 'wife' and 'spouse'. The terms 'boyfriend' and 'girlfriend' should be used with caution because they can be taken to stand for a partner. In past generations people avoided the terms 'girlfriend' or 'boyfriend' and instead talked of 'suitors', 'admirers', 'followers', 'sweethearts' or just 'friends'. The terms 'admirer' and 'suitor' emphasize the fact that a courting couple are 'potential' marriage partners as opposed to actual married partners.

7. Do not use the immoral terms of the relationship culture
In modern times people use phrases like 'I pulled a man', 'I've found a lover', 'I'm hooked up', 'I'm shacked up' and 'I had a one-night stand'. Such terms used to be used only by prostitutes, but now they are commonly used by people who have relationships. The term 'shacked up' means to be living with someone and sharing the same bed. Men who use prostitutes speak of the women being 'cheap' or 'fast'; again, these words are now used by some people in relationships. When a person has a 'one-night stand' involving sex it differs little from a prostitute having a one-night meeting with her customer. Seeing how some of the terminology of the relationship culture has its roots in prostitution can be another motivation to avoid relationships.

8. Be careful with friendships with the opposite sex
The topic of courtship raises the general question of what kinds of friendships there can be with members of the opposite sex. It is a good thing to get to know people of the opposite sex, but it is important not to form close friendships that become exclusive, because that can lead to dangerous misunderstandings.

A situation sometimes arises in which a young man becomes friendly with a particular young woman and the woman assumes that the man is interested in her because of the amount of attention being paid. However, the young man does not actually have any interest in courtship and so there is the danger of the woman being hurt when she finally realizes that the friendship is not actually courtship. Of course, the same can happen the other way round if a man thinks that a woman is interested in him because of a friendship that is getting exclusive. Both men and women should, therefore, be very sensitive to the messages they are giving to members of the opposite sex in friendships.

9. Beware of ungodly entertainment

The apostle Paul warns that bad company can be corrupting for Christians (1 Cor. 15:33). The entertainment we choose to watch can be a very influential friend, so it is important to choose entertainment carefully. When watching the world's entertainment day after day it can be very tempting to think it is fine to give your heart and body away before marriage because everyone else is living that way in modern society. However, Christians are called to walk according to God's Word and not to be conformed to the way of the world. Courtship is an area where Christians should be clearly different from the world.

The Bible teaches that we should choose that which is pure, noble and right (Phil. 4:8). Most secular pop music promotes the relationship culture, and so discernment is very important in the area of popular music. The majority of television soaps and romcoms promote the relationship culture and so are not recommended. There are helpful Christian websites produced by organizations such as The Dove Foundation that can be used to help select wholesome entertainment.[3]

Notes

1 **Joel James,** *Help! I'm Confused about Dating* (Wapwallopen, PA: Shepherd Press, 2011).

2 **Joshua Harris,** *Boy Meets Girl: Say Hello to Courtship* (Sisters, OR: Multnomah, 2005). **Sarah Mally,** *Before You Meet Prince Charming: A Guide to Radiant Purity* (Marion, IA: Tomorrow's Forefathers, 2006).

3 The Dove Foundation, www.dove.org.

SEX OUTSIDE OF
MARRIAGE IS ALWAYS
SELFISH IF WE CONSIDER
THE FEELINGS OF A
FUTURE SPOUSE.

4. God's way: abstain from sexual immorality

Key biblical principle: 'ABSTAIN FROM SEXUAL IMMORALITY' (1 THES. 4:3)

In the context of courtship, abstaining from sexual immorality involves abstaining from all sexual intimacy before marriage. The reason why a person consciously has to abstain is because human nature makes people desire sexual pleasures before marriage. For those who follow the biblical command to abstain there are blessings of a happier marriage or a happier single life.

Young people sometimes ask, 'How far can I go in intimacy with my girlfriend/boyfriend?' But that is the wrong question. The right question is, 'How pure can I be in courtship?' And the answer to that question is that you should abstain from all sexual intimacy in courtship.

I once gave a talk at a church in England and was hosted by a church elder. When I was collected from the station, the elder apologized in advance for his home being in a state of chaos. He explained he had just a few weeks to arrange a wedding because his Christian daughter, who was single and at university, had just announced she was pregnant. Even though she was courting a Christian young man, they had had premarital sex.

Sadly, the above story is becoming increasingly common among Christians. There are some Christians who believe that it is fine to have a degree of sexual intimacy outside of marriage. They then find it difficult not to progress over time to sexual intercourse. This chapter gives six biblical reasons why people should abstain from sexual intimacy outside of marriage.

1. The command to abstain from sexual immorality

Abstain from sexual immorality (1 Thes. 4:3).

In the New Testament the terms 'sexual immorality' and 'fornication' come from the Greek word *porneias*, which refers to any kind of immoral sexual conduct, not just sexual intercourse outside of marriage. Any sexual activity between a man and a woman outside of marriage is sinful because there is no promise of lifelong commitment. When two unmarried people engage in sexual intimacy, such as intimate kissing or groping, this constitutes sexual immorality.

The command to abstain from sexual immorality is given many times in the Bible. The apostle Paul mentions it three times (1 Cor. 6:18; Eph. 5:3; 1 Thes. 4:3). The Jerusalem Council gave a command to abstain from sexual immorality in Acts 15:29. The apostle Peter commands Christians to 'abstain from fleshly lusts', which would certainly include sexual immorality (1 Peter 2:11). Jesus gave a command to abstain from lustful thoughts (Matt. 5:28) and commanded a woman to abstain from adultery (John 8:11). In the Old Testament, the book of Proverbs contains many warnings to avoid sexual immorality (Prov. 5–7). The fact that sexual immorality is mentioned so many times shows that abstinence is really important.

In past generations that respected biblical standards people were expected to abstain from sexual activity before marriage. Sometimes the term 'chastity' was used to describe a life of sexual purity before marriage. Sadly, the world no longer believes in abstinence outside of marriage and so there is great peer pressure for people to behave in an immoral way. However, Christians are to be different from the world.

Authors such as Joshua Harris, Elisabeth Elliot, Heather Paulsen, Sarah Mally and Joel James have all been correct to define sexual immorality as any sexual activity outside of marriage. Joshua Harris chose *Not Even a Hint* as the title for one of his books[1] because the apostle Paul teaches in Ephesians that Christians should not have even a hint of sexual immorality (Eph. 5:3). Elisabeth Elliot chose *Passion and Purity* as the title for one of her books[2] because, while courtship can have passion, there should be complete sexual purity.

In contrast to the above authors, there are now some Christian authors writing that when two Christians are in a relationship they can have a degree of sexual intimacy such as intimate kissing and groping. These authors claim that each person can draw his or her own boundaries about how far to go in physical

54

intimacy. The implied message is that, apart from sexual intercourse, almost any kind of sexual activity is acceptable.

However, the Bible nowhere teaches that people can define their own moral boundaries, and the Bible nowhere teaches that sexual immorality relates only to sexual intercourse. Some may argue that Christians have liberty and freedom to set their own moral boundaries, but the Bible warns against using liberty as an excuse to sin (1 Peter 2:16; Gal. 5:13).

Interestingly, books that advocate a degree of sexual intimacy do not present any biblical justification and avoid the many passages of Scripture that call for abstinence from sexual immorality. There are also obvious difficulties with the unbiblical teaching that a degree of sexual intimacy is fine. How can two people stop themselves from deepening their sexual intimacy over a period of time? Does the woman submit to the man if he demands a higher level of sexual intimacy? How far can groping go before it is deemed sexual immorality? If people have had sexual experiences before marriage, how can they stop that from affecting their marriage? Such questions illustrate the folly of arguing that a degree of sexual intimacy before marriage is acceptable.

Another false teaching that has been proposed in recent times is that sexual intimacy is fine outside of marriage as long as it is 'selfless'. This teaching is dangerous because it encourages people to think that the legitimacy of sexual activity is defined by a 'selflessness' test rather than by a biblical test. People will always want to claim that their actions are not selfish and so will seek to have sexual intimacy before marriage.

In reality, there is no such thing as selfless sex outside of marriage because there is no lifelong covenant. Sex outside of marriage is always selfish if we consider the feelings of a future spouse. Of course, sex should be selfless within marriage, but the point here is that sexual activity should always be *within* marriage.

Interestingly, people who argue that Christians can have a degree of sexual intimacy if they are in a relationship must also argue that the relationship is deep enough to justify sexual intimacy. But if the relationship is that deep, it must be a marriage-like relationship. And if it is a marriage-like relationship, it is dishonouring to marriage because it is an alternative to marriage. So whichever way you analyse sexual relationships, they are not consistent with biblical teaching.

2. The warning about fornication

> Marriage is honorable among all, and the bed undefiled; but fornicators and adulterers God will judge (Heb. 13:4).

Hebrews 13:4 also makes it clear that all sexual activity outside of marriage is immoral. It is not just adulterers who commit sexual immorality but also fornicators. Fornicators include unmarried people who engage in sexual activity before marriage.

A key problem with the modern relationship culture is that it leads people to think that 'being in a relationship' makes it morally fine to give away their bodies. Even though sexual touching like petting and intimate kissing does not involve giving away the body completely, it nevertheless involves giving away the body to some extent.

It is important to realize that intimate kissing and intimate touching are types of sexual foreplay that are designed to lead to sexual intercourse. An intimate kiss can make two people ready for sexual intercourse in a matter of seconds, so abstaining from full sex can be extremely difficult. Countless unwanted pregnancies started with what was meant to be 'just a kiss'.

People who argue that intimate kissing and intimate touching are fine are basically saying that people can start a process of having sex but must not go all the way. But to assume that people always have the ability to stop going all the way is very naive. Sexual desires are among the most powerful passions in a human being and so sexual activity is hard to stop once it has been started. This is why Scripture says that playing with sexual immorality is like playing with fire.

3. Intimate kissing is a sexual pleasure for marriage only

> Let him kiss me with the kisses of his mouth—
> For your love is better than wine …
> Your lips, O my spouse,

Drip as the honeycomb;
Honey and milk are under your tongue …
And the roof of your mouth [is] like the best wine
(S. of S. 1:2; 4:11; 7:9).

There is obviously nothing wrong when two single people give each other a brief kiss on the cheek as a welcome gesture in the same way that friends and family kiss each other as a greeting. However, a lingering sexually intimate kiss with the lips and tongue is a completely different matter because it is a sexual activity. Since intimate kissing is a sexual pleasure, it should be reserved for marriage. One of the reasons why people ask the question 'Have you had your first kiss yet?' is because the first intimate kiss is a very emotional experience. Since first sexual experiences are special, they should be saved for marriage.

It is very clear from the Song of Solomon that intimate kissing is a sexual pleasure for marriage only. Even though there is much symbolism about Christ and the church in the Song of Solomon, the book still describes different pleasures that married people have. In 1:2 it is clear that an intimate kiss is a way of a husband and wife having sexual intimacy. The pleasure of kissing with the lips and tongue is expressed in intimate detail in the Song of Solomon in verses such as 4:11 and 7:9. These verses show that an intimate kiss can be a very sensual and intimate act.

The teaching about lust in Matthew 5:28 is also relevant to intimate kissing. When two unmarried people engage in sexual activities such as intimate kissing there is always lust involved. The whole point of intimate kissing is to experience sexual feelings, so it cannot be argued that intimate kissing can take place without lust.

Note on the world's view of intimate kissing

It is important to point out that secular society considers intimate kissing to be a significant sexual activity. In fact, intimate kissing is considered by law to be a sexual act. If an adult has an intimate kiss on the lips with a minor, he or she can be convicted of a serious sexual crime. The crime is so serious that the adult may receive custodial sentence and may have to be on the sex offenders' register for life. It is also a criminal offence for a man to force a woman to have an intimate kiss. Some Christians have tried to justify intimate kissing on the basis that it is not a significant sexual act. However, it is hard to argue that intimate kissing is not a significant sexual act when even secular society considers it to be a sexual activity with very serious legal consequences under certain circumstances.

Society considers intimate kissing to be one of the most important milestones in a person's life. A person's first intimate kiss is considered a very significant event which he or she will remember for the rest of his or her life. Society is fascinated by statistics such as when people have their first kiss. What is allowable in public places also shows that intimate kissing is a significant sexual activity. In public swimming pools and cinemas kissing is prohibited because other people find it offensive. This ban on intimate kissing demonstrates that it is a significant sexual activity.

Note on engagement

Even though an engaged couple are pledged to be married, they should still abstain from sexual activity until marriage. While it could be argued that intimate kissing is less immoral during engagement because of the expectation of future lifelong commitment, it is still not the biblical ideal and it can lead to the temptation for more sexual activity. Also, if the engagement is broken for some reason, the two people will have regrets about having experienced intimate kissing. One reason why long engagements are not recommended is that they lead to the temptation to start sexual activity.

4. Sexual touching is for marriage only

> It is good for a [an unmarried] man not to touch a woman (1 Cor. 7:1).

There are several Bible verses that show that sexual touching is for marriage only. Proverbs 5:19 describes the sexual touching of a woman's breasts that is clearly only wholesome when it is by a woman's husband. The Song of Solomon describes sexual touching by a married couple (S. of S. 2:6), and there is again the implication that such touching should take place only within marriage.

In 1 Corinthians 7:1 Paul says it is right for an unmarried man not to touch a woman in a sexual way. Then in 1 Corinthians 7:2 Paul goes on to say that to avoid sexual immorality people should get married. The clear implication is that when an unmarried man touches a woman in a sexual way it constitutes sexual immorality. Paul does not say that to avoid sexual immorality you should have relationships.

It is common to hear of a girl saying that she felt dirty after petting with her boyfriend. Even some non-Christians who have no knowledge of biblical principles talk of feeling guilty about sexual activity outside of marriage. The reason why people feel dirty after petting is because such activities are sinful outside of marriage. Over time a person's conscience can become hardened and he or she may lose those feelings of guilt. However, the guilt still accumulates and becomes a type of baggage that people carry through their lives unless they know forgiveness through the Lord Jesus.

As with intimate kissing, sexual touching is considered a sexual act by the legal system. If a man touches a woman's breasts, thighs or bottom without her consent, he can be convicted of serious sexual assault. It is very hard for a Christian to argue that groping of breasts is not a sexual activity when even modern secular society considers such touching a very significant sexual act.

5. Virginity is precious and should be preserved until marriage

if ... evidences of virginity are not found for the young woman ... she has done a disgraceful thing (Deut. 22:20–21).

Deuteronomy 22 illustrates that virginity is a very precious thing for a man and a woman to have on their wedding day. God has designed women with a hymen to show whether they are virgins on their wedding day. When a woman loses her virginity, the hymen is broken and there is significant bleeding which stains the bed sheets.

Deuteronomy 22 describes the situation when a man finds that his bride has not produced any blood on the sheets and therefore there is evidence that she is not a virgin. In such cases the man was expected to detest his bride because of her shameful conduct in having premarital sex. The punishment for not being a virgin in such cases was death. Because of the seriousness of the accusation, the elders were to review the evidence. One of the reasons for the need to review the evidence was because the hymen can sometimes be broken when there has been no sexual activity.

Thankfully, because of the grace that came with the Lord Jesus, such punishments are no longer administered. However, this example given in the Old Testament illustrates the seriousness of the sin of premarital sex and the importance of saving oneself for marriage. Of course, it is equally precious for a man to be a virgin on his wedding day.

The fact that God has designed a woman to have a virginity sign emphasizes that virginity is something precious. In past societies that followed biblical standards, chastity was considered to be very important. If a woman was not a virgin on her wedding day, she was said to have lost her honour and beauty. Modern society has rejected such standards and it is now considered normal to engage in sexual activity from a young age and not to be a virgin on one's wedding day.

Despite the modern drive for sexual freedom, sometimes there is a desire to appear pure on one's wedding day. In recent years there has been a rise in the number of 'virginity repair' operations in which women have surgery to repair their hymens so that on their wedding nights they bleed and make their husbands believe they are virgins. It has been reported that thousands of women in the UK are having this done each year.[3] This shows that, when people get to the point of being married, many like the idea of marrying a virgin or being a virgin.

6. Close affection is for marriage only

Let the husband render to his wife the affection due her, and likewise also the wife to her husband (1 Cor. 7:3).

From this verse it can be seen that physical affection is an important marital pleasure that a husband and wife have a duty to give to each other. The marriage ceremony includes the words 'to have and to hold' because married people have a duty and a privilege to be very affectionate to each other. It follows from 1 Corinthians 7:3 that close physical affection is for marriage only.

The right boundaries of affection when going out with someone are the same as those for a brother–sister relationship (1 Tim. 5:2). In a brother–sister relationship it is fine to have a brief hug and brief kiss on the cheek, so that is also fine when going out with someone. However, a brother and sister would not kiss intimately on the lips or touch each other's bottom, so that is not appropriate during courtship. During courtship it is helpful to continually think to yourself, 'Would I do this with my brother/sister?'

People sometimes use the phrase 'they are all over each other' of people who show a great deal of romantic affection towards each other. People who court should not have that phrase applied to them. In past ages that respected biblical standards of courtship it was considered inappropriate for people to show close affection during courtship. Faithful screen adaptations of period novels show clearly that people who were courting would show no close affection.

Notes

1 **Joshua Harris,** *Not Even a Hint: A Study Guide for Men* (Sisters, OR: Multnomah, 2004).

2 **Elisabeth Elliot,** *Passion and Purity: Learning to Bring Your Love Life under God's Control* (Milton Keynes: Authentic, 2011).

3 *Daily Mail,* 29 July 2010, online.

THINKING ABOUT GIVING
A GIFT OF PURITY TO
YOUR FUTURE SPOUSE
CAN BE A POWERFUL
MOTIVATION TO
EXERCISE SELF-CONTROL
IN COURTSHIP.

5. How to abstain from sexual immorality

Key biblical principle: Christians can do all things through Christ who strengthens them (Phil. 4:13)

Some people argue that it is too idealistic to ask single people to abstain from all physical intimacy, such as intimate kissing. However, God would not command abstention from sexual immorality if it was impossible. The Bible promises that we can do all things through Christ (Phil. 4:13) and that God's grace is sufficient in all situations (2 Cor. 12:9). We should also remember that God does not allow us to be tempted beyond what we can bear (1 Cor. 10:13). Such promises show that God does intervene in our lives to help us. Even though we are all weak by nature, we can be confident of God's help and strength.

In 2013 I led a weekend houseparty for the Loughborough University Christian Union where courtship was one of the topics. I was very encouraged by the students' desire to keep purity in courtship, but they said it was hard when there is such peer pressure to have relationships with physical intimacy. They also said that there was even peer pressure in some churches to have relationships. I explained to the students that there were several practical things they could do to help preserve their sexual purity. I also explained that it was important to pray and to seek help from God. This chapter gives eleven ways to help preserve sexual purity before marriage.

1. Avoid temptation by abstaining from marriage-like relationships
One of the most important ways to abstain from sexual immorality is to abstain from relationships. Having relationships increases temptation because, when two people belong to each other, there is a strong natural urge for them to give their bodies to each other. Young men in particular have powerful sexual urges that are very difficult to control if love is awakened.

The rise in promiscuity in Western society over the last fifty years demonstrates that the relationship culture inevitably encourages sexual activity before marriage.

It is interesting to note that Christian authors who advocate relationships also tend to advocate sexual intimacy outside of marriage. This shows that relationships and sexual intimacy go hand-in-hand.

2. Aim to court late and marry young

In 1 Corinthians 7:9 Paul says of unmarried people, 'if they cannot exercise self-control, let them marry'. One of the key solutions to sexual temptation is to aim to marry young. Church ministers sometimes give the advice 'Court late and marry young'. People should court late so that they are old enough to marry when they start courting. And they should desire to marry young so that they do not get tempted to have a series of relationships before marriage. Of course, it is not always possible to marry young if you cannot find a spouse, but there are definite advantages in having that aim.

Nowadays it is common to hear the advice that people should not marry young. As a consequence, some young people avoid getting married even when they are courting someone they would like to marry. However, by avoiding marriage they are increasing the temptation to sexual immorality because it is very hard to abstain from sexual activity when marriage seems far away in the future. So it is good to seek to marry young to avoid temptation. Of course, it is not easy to take on the responsibilities of marriage—but waiting until you are older does not necessarily make it any easier to take on those responsibilities.

3. Remember the teaching of Scripture

God's Word should be one of the most important motivations for a Christian to live in a God-honouring way. The psalmist said that he had hidden God's word in his heart that he might not sin (Ps. 119:11). Thinking about the Bible's teaching on marriage should motivate Christians to save themselves for marriage. Remembering the many commands to avoid sexual immorality should be further motivation to avoid relationships and sexual intimacy.

4. Pray for self-control

Abstinence requires self-control, so it is important to pray for this important fruit of the Spirit. The man should make it his duty to protect the purity of the woman he is courting. Faithfulness is needed because there should be faithfulness to a future spouse. Patience is also needed because a Christian should be prepared to wait until marriage for the pleasures of marriage. As well as practising self-control, it is also important to avoid tempting situations, such as meeting late at night in a private room all alone.

5. Think of the gift of purity to your future spouse

Thinking about giving a gift of purity to your future spouse can be a powerful motivation to exercise self-control in courtship. During courtship it is helpful to constantly remember that the other person may not be your future spouse and so you should not give away your purity or take away his or her purity. It is helpful to think of questions like: 'How would my future spouse feel if I was to engage in sexual activity with this person during courtship?'

When a Christian avoids relationships before marriage, it makes first sexual experiences very special in marriage. In contrast, the relationship culture cheapens sex and intimacy. No Christian on his or her wedding day ever regrets not having had more relationships or more sexual experiences before marriage; but many Christians do regret the relationships they had before they were married.

When people start having relationships, they often do not realize that every time they have a failed relationship they are getting less attractive for marriage. Some single Christians in the USA wear purity rings to show that they are saving themselves for marriage and are not having relationships or sex before marriage. The use of the purity ring shows that godly Christians want to know who is staying pure before marriage.

Sadly, modern society does not give value to purity. Every soap and film promotes sex and relationships outside of marriage and does not value purity. When celebrities go through many failed relationships, the media makes little reference to the fact that they are becoming less attractive. The prime focus of the media is on external beauty. The message given to society is that purity is not valuable.

I know from personal experience in my teenage years that it is wrong and unfulfilling to have a marriage-like relationship before marriage. During this time I knew that love without lifelong commitment was not right, even though I was not a Christian. When I became a Christian at the age of nineteen I knew forgiveness for my actions but realized I needed to have a change of lifestyle by avoiding relationships. When I married at the age of twenty-five I had had a period of six years of purity, which I found very helpful for my marriage.

6. Remember that you may be asked about past sexual experiences

When giving talks on courtship to groups of young people, I get them to imagine the following scenario in order to make them realize some of the possible consequences of sexual immorality. Imagine a man is courting a woman, and the woman asks him if he has had past sexual relationships. If the man has had past sexual relationships, he has a choice. Either he lies about his past, or he explains his past, with the risk that the woman will not want to marry him. Of course, the above scenario can also happen the other way round, with a man asking a woman about her past sexual experiences. Realizing that past sexual experiences may be a hindrance to getting a future spouse can be a powerful motivation to staying pure before marriage.

If you do have a romantic history to reveal to the other person, it is important to put everything into a spiritual context. If you had sexual experiences before becoming a Christian and explain that to the person you are courting, then, in most cases, he or she will not see that as a hindrance to marriage. If you have had sexual experiences as a Christian and explain that you have repented, many Christians will not see that as an impediment to marriage. The psalmist David was guilty of sexual immorality and knew complete forgiveness, and that is an encouragement to Christians who have fallen in this area. However, despite these reassurances, it is still important to remember that, in some cases, a prospective spouse may be put off by your past sexual experiences.

7. Avoid nightclubs and discos

An important biblical principle is to avoid temptation, and the Bible applies this principle to the area of sexual immorality. Proverbs advises the wise man to steer clear of the place of the prostitute (Prov. 5:8). By staying away from her, he will not see her and be seduced by her looks and perfume. In modern society a Christian should stay away from nightclubs and discos to avoid the temptation to have intimate relationships.

Nightclubs and discos bring together many of the ingredients of the relationship culture in one place, including pop music, immoral dress, immoral dancing, alcohol and lust. The dark room, flashing lights, sensual dress and racy music are

66

all designed to create lustful feelings. The fact that clubs and discos open late at night adds to the seductive atmosphere. Proverbs speaks of how an immoral woman will make her house seductive to attract men (Prov. 7:15–18) and how she works late at night (7:9). Many nightclubs and discos follow this pattern.

There are parallels between nightclubs and discos and the 'far country' which is described in the parable of the prodigal son (Luke 15:11–32). Young people sometimes yearn for nightclubs and discos in the same way that the prodigal son yearned for the far country. Young men sometimes spend their money and time on seductively dressed women in the same way that the prodigal son spent some of his money on prostitutes. And nightclubs and discos involve expensive prodigal living that can make those who frequent them very poor.

In previous generations it was very rare to hear of Christians attending nightclubs or discos. However, in recent times the number of young Christians who attend such places has been growing because of the way the relationship culture has entered the church. As soon as a Christian accepts the standards of the relationship culture, it is inevitable that he or she will be attracted to immoral places like nightclubs that promote relationships.

8. Abstain from seductive clothing and body markings

The Bible teaches that it is a sin to seduce (Prov. 5:20). Some Christian women do not realize that a bare waist, short skirt, tight-fitting clothing or skimpy underwear can tempt men to look lustfully at them. When a man looks lustfully at a woman in sensual clothing, it is not just the man who has done wrong. The woman has also done wrong by tempting men to look lustfully at her. It is important for Christian women to dress discreetly, especially in church services. If a young man sees an attractive lady in revealing clothing in church, it becomes very hard for him to focus on the worship of God.

While tattoos are not inherently wrong, they are immoral if they are seductive. When a woman places tattoos around the edges of her bikini for public view, this is immoral because it encourages men to stare and lust after sensual parts of her body. In the 2003 film *Cheaper by the Dozen* there is a scene where a young man looks lustfully at a young woman in a bikini after his attention is drawn to a tattoo near her bikini. Such scenes in films give the immoral message that tattoos are desirable for women to have because they increase their sex appeal.

While body piercings are not inherently wrong, they too can be inappropriate when they are designed to seduce. The problem with having piercings in places like the navel or tongue is that they invite people to stare at sensual parts of the body.

Sadly, we live in a world that does not give credit to women who are of a gentle and quiet spirit and are modestly dressed. But Christians are to be different, and women who are gentle in spirit and who dress modestly are to be commended.

9. Abstain from pornography

Saving yourself for marriage involves not just avoiding relationships but also avoiding pornography. It is important to realize that pornography includes things that modern society does not recognize as pornography. Most of modern society would not classify pictures of topless women and women in lingerie as pornography, but this certainly is pornography when judged by biblical standards. Job once said, 'I have made a covenant with my eyes; why then should I look upon a young woman?' (Job 31:1). The promise made by Job thousands of years ago that he would not look upon a young woman is very apt for today.

An article in *Psychology Today* in October 2011[1] reported that many men were becoming impotent in their twenties as a direct consequence of having used pornography. The use of pornography was desensitizing them to sexual attraction, so they were aroused only by extreme pornographic material. Ironically, some people think that abstention and purity mean missing out, when actually the opposite is true. People who have sexual experiences before marriage are the ones who are more likely to have less enjoyment in sex during marriage.

When giving talks on pornography to young people I sometimes describe the following scenario. A man is courting a woman and the woman asks him if he has looked at pornography. If the man has done so, either he will lie about his past, or he will explain his past, with the risk that the woman will not want to marry him. Some people might think that asking a man about pornography is too intrusive. However, given that watching pornography can have a very significant effect on a man's ability to be a good husband, it is not unreasonable for a woman to ask such a question. Realizing that pornography can adversely affect a person's ability to get a future spouse can be a powerful motivation to avoid pornography.

The issue of pornography raises the question of whether a Christian (particularly a Christian woman) should ask a man whether he has looked at pornography. This is a personal decision and depends on the individual circumstances. However, I would recommend that women do think seriously about asking this question. Pornography can be very destructive to a marriage. If you met a man who obviously had a gambling problem, you would think very carefully about accepting a proposal of marriage from him. Likewise, if you knew that a man had an addiction to pornography, you would think carefully about marrying him. The problem with an addiction to pornography, however, is that it can be completely hidden. So there is an argument for probing as to whether a prospective husband has a weakness for pornography.

10. Remember that it is never too late to change

As mentioned in the Preface, if you have a history of relationships it is not too late to change and you can still have a period of purity before you get married. To have a period of purity is better than having none. There are many people who committed sexual immorality as non-Christians and then abstained from sexual immorality as Christians. These Christians have found that having a period of purity is still an important gift to give their future spouse. For Christians who have committed sexual immorality, there is still the chance to have a period of purity before marriage.

11. Remember the blessings of purity

There is an important biblical promise that God honours those who honour Him through faith and obedience (1 Sam. 2:30). When a person chooses not to follow the relationship culture, God will honour that path of faith and obedience. A publication by *Family Life* magazine entitled *20 Good Reasons Why Not to Cohabit before Marriage*[2] says it is an established fact that those who are virgins on their wedding day have a much lower chance of divorce, will have a happier marriage and will enjoy sex far more than those who have had sex before marriage. It is just as true that people who avoid having a degree of sexual intimacy before marriage are more likely to have a happy marriage.

Notes

1 **Marnia Robinson and Gary Wilson,** 11 July 2011, 'Porn-Induced Sexual Dysfunction Is a Growing Problem', *Psychology Today,* http://www.psychologytoday.com/blog/cupids-poisoned-arrow/201107/porn-induced-sexual-dysfunction-is-growing-problem.

2 By **Don Weston** (Kansas City, MO: Family Life Ministries—Church of the Nazarene, 1998).

RELATIONSHIPS CAN
HINDER MATURITY
BECAUSE THEY GIVE
PEOPLE AN EXCUSE NOT
TO GET READY FOR THE
RESPONSIBILITIES OF
MARRIED LIFE.

6. How relationships are dangerous

Key biblical principle: SEXUAL IMMORALITY IS DANGEROUS

The Bible has many warnings about the harmful consequences of sexual immorality. Sexual intimacy outside of marriage is always dangerous because it goes against God's design that romance should be within marriage. The book of Proverbs warns that it is like playing with fire (Prov. 6:27); it can take away that person's soul (6:32); and it can lead him or her down to hell (7:27). Hosea says that sexual immorality enslaves the heart (Hosea 4:11). The New Testament also has several warnings about sexual immorality. The apostle Paul teaches that sexual immorality is serious because it is a sin against the body. He says it is a sin that Christians should flee from (1 Cor. 6:18), and that a Christian should not keep company with a brother who is committing sexual immorality (1 Cor. 5:11). In 1 Corinthians 10:8 he records that 23,000 people died because of sexual immorality. One of the sins of the seven churches in Revelation was sexual immorality (Rev. 2:20). Understanding the seriousness of the consequences of sexual immorality is a helpful motivation to maintaining sexual purity.

It is vital to realize that marriage provides important protection, especially for women, by ensuring that a man and a woman are fully committed before becoming joined together. In contrast, relationships have no such protection and tempt people to use relationships for selfish and even abusive ends.

Relationships seem so appealing to teenagers that they are often impatient to have their first relationship and first intimate kiss. However, young people are often unaware that relationships have many harmful consequences. When Christians have relationships, they suffer the same harmful consequences as non-Christians.

Of course, following biblical standards of courtship gives no guarantee of avoiding these dangers. However, problems are much less likely to arise when there is no sexual activity and there are no relationship splits.

1. The Bible warns that sexual immorality is dangerous

Even though many of the warnings given in Proverbs 5–7 mention adultery and prostitution, they are nevertheless fully relevant to any type of sexual immorality. A person who watches pornography, dresses in a sexually seductive way or has intimate relationships is also subject to the warnings of Proverbs 5–7. A sexual relationship outside of marriage creates such powerful emotions and attachments that it is as dangerous as playing with fire.

The examples of King David, Samson and Solomon show that sexual immorality has very serious consequences even for godly and wise people. David was one of the most powerful kings, Samson was the strongest man ever and Solomon the wisest man ever. Yet all three experienced great problems because of their sexual immorality. The warnings of Scripture concerning sexual immorality should be a powerful motivation for Christians to avoid relationships.

In contrast to the Bible, the world does not warn people about the dangers of relationships. One of the lies of the devil is that having sexual pleasures outside of marriage has no adverse consequences. The entertainment industry promotes that lie on a daily basis in the way that actors are shown getting away with immoral behaviour in films and plays. Films show countless incidences of promiscuous sex but there is virtually no mention of unwanted pregnancies, broken families, broken lives and sexually transmitted diseases (STDs). According to Hollywood films, people in relationships suffer few consequences from their lifestyle. Yet in Western countries such as the USA, over a third of adults have contracted STDs, due mainly to the relationship culture.

In December 2011 the UK Schools Minister, Nick Gibb, said that one of the problems of modern society is the 'have it now' culture, because it can lead to debt and a lifetime of financial problems. The 'have it now' culture can also be seen in the relationship culture. The relationship culture encourages people to have marital pleasures now rather than waiting until marriage for the pleasures of marriage. And the relationship culture can lead to a lifetime of emotional problems.

2. Relationship splits are traumatic

One of the most harmful consequences of relationships is the emotional damage that comes through relationship splits. Divorce is an emotionally violent activity (Mal. 2:16) and so it is inevitable that relationship break-ups are traumatic and cause a trail of damage in people's lives. The emotional trauma of relationship splits can manifest itself in many ways, including anger, regret, blame, recriminations and accusations.

In my role as a university Senior Tutor I have been responsible for giving pastoral support to the students who are most in need. One of the most common reasons for students being in serious need is relationship splits. Students often ask to see me to explain how they are suffering the trauma of a failed relationship. Some students are so badly affected that they are sure they cannot continue with their studies. Other students are so heartbroken they feel suicidal. Helping these students back on their feet is a challenging task.

One reason why relationship splits are painful is because when you have given your heart to someone, it can be very hard to stop loving that person. And when someone else had given his or her heart to you, it can be difficult to accept that he or she has withdrawn that pledge of love. It is very common to hear of a young person in great distress over the ending of a relationship. Even the most hard-hearted person can be devastated by a relationship split. Relationship splits can be so traumatic that many people attempt suicide. Around 140,000 people attempt suicide each year in the UK, and relationship splits are one of the most common causes. Avoiding relationships is the way to avoid the devastating heartache of divorce-like experiences.

Of course, courtship can be very disappointing if it does not lead to marriage, but the pain is on a completely different level because there is no tearing apart of a one-flesh relationship. In addition, there is no withdrawal of pledges of love from another person.

3. Relationship splits can cause widespread damage
I know from personal childhood experience that divorce can be destructive to a family and can create a trail of devastation. Parents can be so absorbed in fighting their ex-spouses and pursuing new relationships that they have little time or energy for their families. Parents and grandparents argue over access to children

and people take sides over who is to blame. In the same way, when a relationship ends, it can lead to widespread problems within a family and a church.

If the two people go to the same church, one or both parties often feel they have to leave. I have seen tensions and divisions in families and churches caused by relationship break-ups. I have also seen people and families leaving churches just because of relationship break-ups. If the two people who have split have mutual friends, there is the awkwardness of these friends having to take sides. In contrast, courtship is much less likely to result in widespread problems because it is carried out discreetly and if it ends without marriage there is no traumatic split.

4. Relationships hinder the process of maturing and growing in faith

Relationships can hinder maturity because they give people an excuse not to get ready for the responsibilities of married life. In past ages, young men matured in their late teens as they prepared to lead and support a family. In contrast, many young men today are more interested in having fun than in developing the maturity necessary for leading a family. In addition, relationships give young men a way of having the pleasures of marriage without actually getting married. In modern society many people admit that they do not feel ready for marriage until they are in their thirties.

Another reason why relationships hinder the development of young people is because relationships are emotionally draining and time-consuming. Teenage years are a time when there should be great development spiritually, physically and intellectually. However, in modern times many young people are underachieving and lacking in maturity because they are being so distracted by relationships. In my work in universities over the last thirty years I have witnessed a general decline in student maturity. Relationships also create family tensions because of the pressures of commitment they put on young people. Teenage years should be a time for enjoying family life, but relationships often create family conflicts and problems.

A great irony of relationships is that they give people a false sense of maturity. A young person who is having relationships is often tempted to feel grown-up and superior to others who have not had relationships. In the same way, people who have had an intimate kiss are tempted to feel more grown-up than others who have not kissed intimately. It is common for schoolchildren to boast to their peers that they are more mature because they have greater experience in romantic relationships. However, the reality is that, when young people start having relationships, this actually hinders the process of maturing.

For a Christian, having relationships can cause not just immaturity in character but also immaturity in faith. Waiting for a marriage partner involves developing faith and reliance on God. In particular, prolonged periods of being single cause a person to rely upon God and develop his or her faith. Romantic relationships hinder a Christian from calling on God.

5. There is a temptation to have relationships with non-Christians

Some Christians say that, even though they would not marry a non-Christian, they would be prepared to date a non-Christian. The justification given for this is that relationships are there for enjoyment, not just for exploring the possibility of marriage. Since enjoyment often means dating someone with good looks, it is inevitable that such Christians will sometimes date non-Christians. As most films portray looks as the most important factor in choosing a partner, it is inevitable that Christians who follow the relationship culture will choose good-looking non-Christians to date.

Another reason given for justifying courting non-Christians is the hope that the other person will be converted. But Paul gives a clear command that Christians should not be yoked with unbelievers (2 Cor. 6:14). When a Christian chooses to marry a non-Christian because he or she is physically attractive, this is a worldly decision that may have negative consequences. One application of Proverbs 12:26 is that non-Christians can lead believers astray. Abraham chose a spouse well and this was one reason why his life was blessed. Lot chose a spouse poorly and this was one reason why his life had limited blessing.

6. Relationships lead to the abuse of teenage girls

Relationships have been found to be directly responsible for violence against teenage girls on a massive scale in Western society. A study undertaken by Bristol University and the NSPCC in the UK found that around a third of girls aged thirteen to seventeen are sexually assaulted or physically assaulted by boys.[1] These figures correspond to millions of girls at any one time in the UK. Of course, it is not always girls who get abused, but the overwhelming trend is for girls to be victims.

In many cases the sexual assault happens because a boy wants to engage in sexual activity against the wishes of his girlfriend. Sometimes sexual abuse comes as part of a reaction to a relationship split. When one party has ended the relationship, the person who is abandoned (or dumped) can feel so angry that he or she considers reacting in a violent way. Proverbs warns that 'jealousy is a husband's fury' (Prov. 6:34), showing that powerful emotions arise when a romantic relationship is under threat. Relationship splits can lead to extreme and irrational behaviour by even the most 'normal' of people.

The statistics relating to the abuse of teenage girls are similar in the USA. Around 32 per cent of high-school students are involved in an abusive relationship and 1 in 7 teenagers have reported threats from their boyfriend or girlfriend to harm them or themselves to avoid a break-up.[2] Many teenagers will be scarred for life as a result of such abuse and it is likely to affect their future marriage, if there is one.

The incidence of serious sexual violence against teenage girls is desperately sad, yet it should not be surprising because Scripture warns that indulging in sex outside of marriage has dangerous consequences. Relationships inevitably create conflicts if one partner (usually the boy or man) wants to engage in more sexual activity than the other partner. Since relationships involve two people belonging to each other to some extent, it is impossible to avoid such conflicts.

7. Relationships lead to the abuse of women

In the UK around 200,000 women are assaulted by their boyfriends each year. In the USA the number is around one million, with the most vulnerable age being twenty to twenty-four.[3] In 2008 it was reported that, on average, two women are killed every week in the UK by a boyfriend/ex-boyfriend or husband/ex-husband. In the USA, around twenty-one women are murdered every week by a boyfriend/ ex-boyfriend or husband/ex-husband. And for every murder, there are many cases of serious injuries inflicted by ex-boyfriends. The main cause of these appalling statistics is the relationship culture.

Some may argue that wife-beating used to be common in past generations and that it was not reported or dealt with. However, the main point here is that there was very little violence in courtship in past generations. The relationship culture has brought violence into the lives of single women before marriage. And while there was undoubtedly some wife-beating in past generations, there is no indication that it was on anything like the scale of violence that exists in the relationship culture today. It could be argued that the relationship culture has increased violence within marriage because people carry the behaviour they had during relationships into marriage.

Some argue that they would never be abusive in a relationship, so it is all right for them to have relationships. However, having relationships means giving support to a culture that inevitably leads to violence against girls and women. One of the most important ways to help stop the abuse of girls and women is to abstain from the relationship culture itself and to encourage others to do the same.

8. Relationships have dangerously vague rules

Even though the term 'relationship' means a kind of marriage, it can have very different levels of seriousness. People sometimes use adjectives to describe the state of the relationship—such as 'steady relationship', 'long-term relationship', 'serious relationship', 'casual relationship', 'on-off relationship', 'online relationship' and 'fun relationship'. People try to keep everyone up-to-date with the current state of their relationship by using the most appropriate adjective. The fact that the term 'relationship' can have so many different meanings shows that relationships are dangerously vague.

The rules of relationships are inherently vague because there is no lifelong commitment. To some people, relationships are casual and can be ended at whim. To other people, relationships are very serious and should not be finished casually. Relationships appeal to human nature because they allow people to make up their own rules and do what is right in their own eyes (Deut. 12:8). In contrast, marriage is always a serious lifelong relationship and people know where they stand. And since courtship is a friendship, people know where they stand with courtship.

The vagueness of the rules of relationships means that it is inevitable that serious conflicts will often arise. At the beginning of a relationship two people can be very content with the way the relationship appears to be going, but that is only because they are unaware of the true expectations of the other person. It is inevitable that disagreements will arise later, such as about how long to wait before having sexual intimacy or when to get engaged and married. The vagueness of relationships plays into the hands of the devil, because he can work in the minds of two people and cause them to have different standards and expectations.

Sometimes the conflict of expectations can have fatal consequences. On 22 February 2008 *The Daily Telegraph* reported that a woman had committed suicide after her boyfriend insisted that she abort their twin babies. Despite having lived together as a couple for several years, the boyfriend was not committed enough to want the babies. In contrast, the girlfriend was fully committed to the relationship, was desperate to keep the babies and could not understand the lack of commitment of her boyfriend. She felt so devastated after the abortion that she committed suicide. In this tragic incident, the pregnancy revealed that the levels of commitment of the two people were completely different.

9. Relationships can be addictive
One characteristic of the modern relationship culture is that it encourages people to constantly seek to be in a relationship and to avoid being single. Since relationships are pursued for pleasure, it is inevitable that people will be tempted to have serial relationships because that is the way of maximizing their 'fun'. Some people seek to have many relationships simply because they like the fun of experiencing a variety of partners. As long as people are not two-timing, modern society says it is fine for them to 'enjoy themselves' by having serial relationships. The modern acceptance of serial relationships is in stark contrast with past societies. A hundred years ago it would have been considered very immoral to have serial romantic relationships.

When a person has an addiction to a sinful pleasure like excessive alcohol, the addiction may be so powerful that he or she continues that addiction despite repeatedly suffering adverse consequences (Prov. 26:11). Hollywood plays a part in keeping people addicted to relationships because film-makers create unrealistic expectations of romantic bliss in the way they portray relationships in films. The devil also has a role in maintaining people's addiction because he can make them hope that their next relationship will be successful, despite the fact that previous relationships have failed.

Relationships can be a powerful addiction because people get such a high from a marriage-type relationship that there is a large emotional void when the relationship ends. Getting the next boyfriend or girlfriend can become an essential fix and there can be the temptation to act on impulse and enter into a new relationship without much caution. It is very common to hear that someone has got a new boyfriend or girlfriend 'on the rebound'. This lack of caution can mean that the next partner is not likely to be a good match and therefore the new relationship is likely to fail. So the cycle goes on, from one doomed relationship to the next.

A particular danger with addictions is that addicts need an ever-increasing stimulus to satisfy themselves and so they cross new lines of extreme behaviour over time. Alcoholics gradually increase the amount they drink in order to satisfy their desire. Drug addicts get more dangerous levels of drugs to satisfy their need. Similarly, those having relationships go further and further in their sexual experience in order to seek satisfaction.

10. People get entangled in relationships

People become entangled in relationships because, as soon as they officially declare themselves boyfriend and girlfriend, they become emotionally attached and under pressure to meet the needs of the other person. Compared with lifelong marriage, people assume there is not the same need for caution when having relationships. Some people will start a relationship at a party or nightclub with a complete stranger. To assume that there is no need for caution in relationships is of course a mistake. People may think that starting a relationship is not a big deal, but later they find they are so entangled that it is difficult to get out of the relationship.

11. Relationships are an idol in modern society

One test of whether something is an idol is whether it is given prime time in the media. This is certainly true of the relationship culture. Most newspapers and magazines devote many pages to news of celebrity relationships. When high-profile celebrities have a relationship split the news can even make the front page. There are prime-time TV programmes on dating, such as *Take Me Out* (ITV), *Blind Date* (ITV) and *Dinner Date* (ITV). Pop music and Hollywood films encourage an addiction to relationships by making them a dominating theme in entertainment.

The prolific rise of the dating-agency industry shows how much relationships are idolized today. There are numerous dating agencies that advertise through newspapers and on the Internet. Dating websites are one of the most common and most profitable types of website on the Internet. Even websites used by teenagers, such as Facebook, have adverts for dating agencies. People are prepared to spend significant amounts of time and money on the Internet in their bid to get a relationship or to record their relationship on sites like Facebook. Some dating agencies charge up to £10,000 per year for membership.[4]

It is significant that dating is sometimes referred to as a game that people play. A long-running TV programme was entitled *The Dating Game* and magazines often carry articles with that title. Calling dating a game shows that society expects relationships to be pursued primarily for pleasure and as an end in themselves. It also shows that relationships involve people playing with the emotions and lives of others. In contrast to relationships, courtship is never seen as a game but as a serious activity that is undertaken with pure motives. With courtship there is never a sense of winning or losing.

Like any idol, relationships can become all-absorbing. The biggest goal in life can become getting that next boyfriend or girlfriend. Sadly, this urge to date can be seen among some Christians. But Christians should not follow the idols of the world—they should seek first the kingdom of heaven (Matt. 6:33). Understanding how relationships are an idol of modern society should help a Christian to be wary of them.

12. Many people now experience a lifetime of failed relationships

In John 4 there is an account of a woman who had had several failed relationships in her life. The Lord Jesus told this woman that He knew about her five husbands even though He had not met her before. It is clear from the passage that having five relationships represented a path of failure. We now live in a society full of people who, like that woman, have had several failed relationships. This can particularly be seen in the lives of celebrities, but the lifestyle is now becoming common throughout society.

To go through a whole lifetime of failed relationships is a tragic thing. God has designed men and women to have a lifelong relationship with one person of the opposite sex, not to go through a lifetime of failed relationships. It is far better to go through life single than to experience the disappointment of having had many relationships which did not last.

13. How relationships damage society

In past eras, when people followed biblical standards of courtship, there were stable families, low divorce rates, low abortion rates and low levels of sexual immorality. In contrast, the relationship culture has been one of the main reasons for the moral breakdown of society.

Relationships have caused a breakdown of the traditional family because they encourage a culture of divorce and because they make it acceptable to have children outside of marriage. The proportion of births outside of marriage in the UK in 2013 was around 40 per cent; in 1900 it was only about 4 per cent.[5] It is predicted that by 2016 most children will be born out of wedlock. The relationship culture has been the main cause of the huge increase in the number of abortions. Not only does increased sexual activity lead to more unwanted pregnancies, but there is also more likelihood of women wanting an abortion. Since relationships are primarily for pleasure and not to investigate marriage, women are now much more reluctant to go ahead with an unwanted pregnancy.

The relationship culture has been a major factor in encouraging immoral and sensual clothing. Since physical attraction is now seen as a major factor in choosing a date, many women deliberately wear seductive clothing to attract potential partners. The book of Proverbs talks about women who have the attire of a prostitute (Prov. 7:10) and also of the 'seductress' (5:20). In past ages it was only prostitutes who wore provocative clothing in order to seduce passers-by. However, in modern society it is ordinary people who dress to seduce onlookers.

The relationship culture has encouraged the immoral practice of older men divorcing their wives in order to marry much younger women from poor countries. Young brides often come from countries such as Thailand, Russia and the Philippines because poor women are more willing to marry an older richer man in a Western country. The practice of buying young brides from poor countries has been called 'cultural prostitution' because it deprives countries of young women of childbearing age. As often happens with immoral practices, such marriages often fail, causing yet more social instability.

According to present society, the only important rule with relationships is that people should have one partner at a time. But that rule may one day change. On 8 July 2004 a psychology lecturer at University College, Worcester, presented a paper promoting multiple relationships at a meeting of the Lesbian, Gay, Bisexual and Transgender Psychology Group, which is part of the British Psychological Society's Psychology of Women Section Conference in Brighton. A key problem with relationships is that there is no limit to the level of sexual immorality. As soon as society abandons biblical marriage, it is inevitable that there will be a moral decline that will go all the way to the depravity of Sodom and Gomorrah.

On 17 September 2012 Leon Panetta, the United States Defense Secretary, said that the military was sensitive to three issues that plague society: substance abuse, financial distress and relationship problems.[6] Notice how one of the three major problems of society is relationship problems. Even some sections of secular society can recognize that intimate relationships cause great problems.

Notes

1 NSPCC, 1 September 2009, www.nspcc.org.uk.
2 US Bureau of Justice Statistics, 28 June 2013.
3 Ibid.
4 BBC report, 23 February 2011.
5 *Independent,* 16 July 2003.
6 *USA Today,* 17 September 2012.

RELATIONSHIPS TEACH
PEOPLE HOW TO GET
DIVORCED, NOT HOW TO
BE FAITHFUL.

7. How relationships are bad preparation for marriage

Key biblical principle: MARRIAGE INVOLVES UNCONDITIONAL LOVE (EPH. 5:33)

A married couple have the serious responsibility to love each other as their own flesh (Eph. 5:33). A husband has a responsibility to love his wife as Christ loved the church and to provide leadership for the marriage and family (Eph. 5:25). The wife has a responsibility to provide support to her husband (Prov. 31:10–31). To carry out these profound biblical roles requires much preparation and thought. This is why couples are encouraged to attend marriage preparation classes during engagement. In contrast, relationships do not involve unconditional love or other high biblical standards. Relationships are therefore bad preparation for marriage.

In my pastoral work I have had experience of leading marriage preparation classes. These classes involve around ten meetings over a period of several months. Engaged couples have said that it has been very helpful to spend a significant amount of time learning about the biblical roles of a husband and wife before actually getting married. In contrast, people enter into relationships with very little preparation for their relationship roles and end up behaving according to what they observe in Hollywood films or among their friends. There are a number of ways in which relationships are bad preparation for marriage.

1. Relationships are bad preparation for marital roles
Relationships involve people having their own sets of rules which are usually very different from those of biblical marriage. There is no promise by the woman to submit to her boyfriend, and no promise by the man to love his girlfriend as Christ loved the church. Indeed, the world encourages the woman not to submit to her boyfriend, and it does not encourage the man to love his girlfriend as Christ loved the church.

When people have had several relationships before marriage, they will inevitably tend to behave in their marriage as they did in their relationships. If a man has not given unconditional affection in relationships, he will be tempted not to give unconditional affection in marriage. If a person has been rebellious in previous relationships, he or she will tend to be rebellious in marriage. If someone has been argumentative in previous relationships, he or she will tend to be argumentative in marriage.

One key area where single people often get into bad habits is that of gossiping about relationships. It is common for a young dating couple to tell their friends intimate details of their relationship. Indeed, much of the gossip in schools and colleges is fuelled by revelations about relationships. In contrast, a godly marriage involves a married couple being totally loyal to each other in word and deed. A godly husband and wife would never reveal secrets of their marriage without the knowledge of their spouse. When people have gossiped about details of their relationships before marriage, they will be tempted to gossip about their marriage.

Marriage is now often stereotyped as something that does not work very well. Ironically, one of the main reasons why marriage does not work well in modern society is because the relationship culture makes people ill-prepared for marriage.

2. Relationships teach people how to get divorced, not how to be faithful

Marriage involves a lifelong commitment to love the other person (Matt. 5:31–32). Relationships, however, encourage a culture of divorce, because with relationships people are free to leave their partner whenever it suits them. When people experience many relationship splits, they become experts in getting divorced and justifying divorce, and they carry that expertise into marriage. Of course, people hope that when they get married they will 'settle down' and not quit as they did in previous relationships. The reality, however, is that they will be tempted to desire a change of partner just as they did in their relationships.

Marriage vows include a commitment to love 'for better, for worse ... until death us do part'. If your husband or wife becomes seriously ill and weak, you have to stand by his or her side for the rest of his or her life. To keep the vow 'for better, for worse' requires a patient and selfless attitude. In contrast, relationships give permission for people to walk out at any moment. Human nature is such that people do just walk away from relationships for selfish reasons. It is common to hear of relationships where people have walked off because they have 'found a better partner' or because their partner 'lost his/her job' or because their partner 'was always ill'. When people have had many relationships they were able to walk away from when times got tough, they will find it very hard to keep the vow 'for better, for worse' in marriage.

The effect of the relationship culture on marriage can be seen clearly with celebrity marriages. Celebrity marriages often break down after just a few years and the reason is often that the celebrities are not prepared to keep the vow 'for better, for worse'. In some cases celebrity marriages fail in an astonishingly short period. In 2011 Kris Humphries and Kim Kardashian had a marriage that lasted just seventy-two days. In 1994 Drew Barrymore had a marriage with Jeremy Thomas that lasted just nineteen days. One of the shortest celebrity marriages of all was that between Britney Spears and Jason Alexander in 2004, which lasted just fifty-five hours! Celebrities often exhibit arrogance and a lack of patience in their relationships before marriage and this inevitably continues when they get married.

Some people justify the high divorce rates by arguing that marriage has never worked very well and that divorce was rare in the past because of laws against divorce. But this is a false argument. Marriages are often unhappy today because of the effect of relationships. Marriage very often did work well in past generations, when there was no relationship culture.

3. Learning by mistakes is a dangerous philosophy
Modern philosophy argues that young people need to experiment with their sexuality and with relationships so they can learn from their mistakes. But this is a flawed and dangerous philosophy. While a person may occasionally learn a few lessons from failed relationships, there will always be more harm done than good. To say that young people can learn useful things from relationships is like saying that a child can learn useful things from playing on his or her own with matches and fire. Some people argue that they do not feel ready for marriage and therefore want to pursue relationships. However, if a person is not ready for marriage, he or she is not ready for a marriage-like relationship.

When relationships fail, people do not calmly learn lessons and improve. It is human nature to blame other people and to get angry when things go wrong. To argue that a relationship split is a helpful learning process is like saying that experiencing a car crash can be a helpful learning experience for becoming a better car driver. While it might seem plausible that a car crash could be a useful experience in some sense, the reality is that it can lead to serious injuries that give scars for life. In the same way, relationships can give scars for life. The Bible does not say, 'Therefore a man shall leave his father and mother and shall learn how to cope with the trauma of failed relationships and then shall settle down with his wife.'

4. Romantic feelings for an ex-partner can carry on into marriage

Relationships before marriage can do harm to a marriage because it is not easy to blot out all memories of feelings for ex-partners. When someone has 'given his or her heart and body' to another person in a romantic relationship, it is not easy to stop loving that person. And while you may be convinced that you will stop having feelings for your ex-partner, you have no control over whether your ex-partner will stop having feelings for you. It is often the case that one person did not want a relationship to end, and that person in particular can be tempted to retain romantic feelings for his or her ex-partner. This is one of the reasons why marriage should be 'until death us do part'.

One of the reasons why some people have on-off relationships is because they cannot switch off their romantic feelings for the other person. The fact that people sometimes admit that they will 'always have a place in their heart for their ex' shows the enduring emotional power of a relationship. The fact that websites like Friends Reunited often lead to previous romances being rekindled shows that people do not easily forget past relationships. It only takes a certain place or song that had a connection with an ex-partner and it is all too easy to have affectionate feelings for that person again. There is also the problem of comparison. If your ex-partner was better at intimate kissing than your spouse, this can tempt you to be dissatisfied with your spouse. Such thoughts are an act of unfaithfulness to your spouse.

5. There can be awkward meetings with your ex-partner

When two people split, they often assume or hope they will not have to work or socialize together closely in the future. However, the world is surprisingly small and acquaintances from the past sometimes reappear unexpectedly in the workplace or the local church. Such chance meetings can cause unhelpful thoughts and feelings. Imagine a scenario where a married couple are going through a difficult time and one of them regularly bumps into an ex-boyfriend or ex-girlfriend. It can be tempting to look for comfort in such meetings, but that would be dangerous and unfaithful.

ONLY WITH THE
LIFELONG COMMITMENT
OF MARRIAGE AND
BIBLICAL VOWS CAN
TWO PEOPLE ACTUALLY
BECOME SOULMATES.

8. How the relationship culture undermines marriage

Key biblical principle: HONOUR MARRIAGE (HEB. 13:4; GEN. 2:24)

Intimate relationships are dishonouring to marriage because they are an alternative to marriage. When society promotes the relationship culture it is inevitable that marriage will decline, because it is human nature to want the pleasures of marriage without the commitment of marriage. One of the most important ways of honouring marriage is to avoid marriage-like relationships before marriage. In the last decade the church has been vigorously opposed to gay marriage, recognizing that if gay people are allowed to marry it will undermine the institution of marriage. However, the institution of marriage has already been under attack over the last hundred years through the relationship culture.

I have spent many summers visiting Liberty University in the USA, which is the largest Christian university in the world, with over 12,000 students. The university is located in Lynchburg, Virginia, where there is a very strong Christian influence on the local culture. One thing that is very noticeable is that biblical standards of courtship are very common and people have a high respect for marriage and avoid intimate relationships. As a consequence, very few people cohabit and many people marry young. Sadly, most of Western society is dominated by the relationship culture and as a consequence the institution of marriage has been undermined.

1. Relationships are an alternative to marriage

Relationships are an alternative to marriage. When two people have an intimate relationship there are unspoken vows, such as 'I am your partner', 'I belong to you' and 'I will be there for you'. However, there is no vow of lifelong commitment and the vows are not made before God. Relationships are very appealing to human nature because they involve marital pleasures from a young age but without the commitment of lifelong marriage.

In past ages where there was a biblical courtship culture, people had a choice of being married or being single. However, in modern society people have an additional choice of having relationships. As the relationship culture becomes more popular, so the institution of marriage becomes less special and less honoured. Whereas in past societies most people aspired to getting married as young adults, now most people aspire to being in relationships as young adults.

In past ages living together was frowned upon and called 'living in sin'. However, in modern times living together is seen as a legitimate alternative to setting up a marital home. The practice of living together means that marriage is no longer seen as necessary but simply as an optional extra. In fact, marriage is now often seen as an inconvenient optional extra. People today say they cannot get married because it is too expensive or because they would rather spend money on a holiday or a house. Ironically, the reason why marriage is often expensive is because people are living together before marriage and so marriage only seems worthwhile if there is an elaborate wedding.

2. Relationships have caused a decline in the number of people getting married

The relationship culture has resulted in a dramatic decline in the number of people getting married. Since relationships are seen as equivalent to marriage, it should not be surprising that many people see cohabiting as an alternative to marriage. The proportion of the population getting married today is only about half of that in 1900 because many people now choose to cohabit rather than get married.

In 2008 there were around 233,000 weddings in England and Wales, but that figure would have been over 400,000 if the same proportion of society was getting married as in 1900. When you take into account that many modern marriages are actually remarriages following divorce, the actual decline is even greater.

3. Relationships have raised the average age at which people get married

When society has a relationship culture, this always increases the average age at which people get married. One reason is that people want to have the fun of several relationships before settling down. Another reason for the delay in marriage is that the relationship culture makes cohabiting acceptable before marriage.

The increase in the average age at which people marry can be clearly seen over the last hundred years as the relationship culture has become stronger in Western society. The average age at which women get married (for the first time) in the UK has risen from around twenty-three in 1900 to around twenty-nine in 2004. The average age for men has risen from around twenty-five in 1900 to around thirty-one in 2004.

When you consider that a person's healthiest and most vigorous years are their twenties, these increases are very significant. The delay in getting married is a self-reinforcing problem because when men see that the average age for getting married is thirty-one, they are much less prepared to save themselves for marriage than if the average age was twenty-five.

In contrast, when society has a courtship culture, people tend to get married young because there is no alternative to marriage. And when people can see that there is a tendency to marry young, they do not mind saving themselves for marriage—and so there is a virtuous cycle that ensures marriage is honoured. In areas where there is a strong Bible culture, such as Bible Belt areas in the USA, there is still a trend for men and women to marry in their early to mid-twenties.

4. Relationships have been a key reason for the rise in divorce rates

In the last hundred years in the West the number of divorces has increased enormously by a factor of something like 100. The relationship culture is the primary reason for this ungodly trend because the relationship culture makes it sociably acceptable to go through marital splits and remarry. The relationship culture encourages people of all ages to seek new relationships and to believe that lifelong commitment is not important. This is why there are dating agencies that target every age group. The great rise in divorce has resulted in the institution of marriage being greatly undermined.

5. The terminology of relationships is damaging to marriage

As discussed in Chapter 3, relationships dishonour marriage because they copy the language of marriage. In modern society marital terms like 'spouse', 'husband' and 'wife' are discouraged or even banned in order to prevent marriage being seen as superior to relationships. The media tries to use the term 'partner' whether someone is married or not in order to give equal status to people in relationships. On 8 April 2011 a man wrote a letter to *The Daily Telegraph* expressing his surprise and sorrow that he was not allowed to refer to his wife as his 'wife' when he was at the dental surgery. This particular dental practice insisted that everyone refer to spouses as partners, not as husbands or wives. By giving equal status to relationships, the institution of marriage is greatly devalued.

6. The world sees having a soulmate as the ultimate goal of romance

The modern world does not recognize marriage as the ideal place for a romantic relationship. Instead the world judges a relationship in terms of whether two people are 'soulmates'. People now say things like, 'I have found my soulmate' or 'I am looking for my soulmate'. If two unmarried people are soulmates, their relationship is said to be as good as it can be.

Many celebrities and films are now promoting the stereotype that soulmate status is the ultimate criterion for successful romance, rather than marriage. People sometimes use the concept of soulmate to justify past failed relationships by saying that those past relationships failed because they had not found their soulmate. Sadly, many people do not realize that the whole point of marriage is to ensure that two people do actually become soulmates. Only with the lifelong commitment of marriage and biblical vows can two people actually become soulmates.

7. Relationships have devalued purity

In past societies people treasured their purity and wanted to be virgins on their wedding day. The white dress worn at a wedding was always an important sign of purity. Sadly, purity is no longer valued by society and people give away their bodies very cheaply. People today are not embarrassed to say they have had several sexual partners. Nick Clegg, the former Deputy Prime Minister in the UK, told *GQ* magazine in 2011 that he had had fewer than thirty lovers in his life, as if that was a small number.[1]

8. The marriage ceremony is now valued for the trimmings

In Victorian and earlier times a newlywed couple would rarely be cohabiting before marriage. As a consequence, the marriage day focused on the church service and the spiritual significance of the marriage vows. In contrast, it is now expected that people who get married are already living together and the focus of the wedding is on the events after the church service, such as the reception and evening party. While it can be very good to have a lovely reception and evening party, these events should not be seen as more important than the marriage ceremony.

It is common to hear people say that a particular wedding was very special because the reception venue was impressive and there was a great party in the evening. However, what makes a wedding special is the purity of the bride and bridegroom, not the glamour of the parties. When two people have kept their purity before marriage, their wedding is very special even if the trimmings are modest.

9. How leaders and celebrities have devalued marriage

Leaders and celebrities such as top sportsmen and film stars commonly have serial relationships outside of marriage and cohabit outside of marriage. In 2010 Ed Milliband became the first Leader of the Opposition in the UK to be cohabiting with his girlfriend. The press reported this as an entirely acceptable way to live. Many people see leaders and celebrities as role models whom they want to copy. Sadly, leaders and celebrities have set a bad example by their lifestyle and have devalued marriage.

The change in standards in society can be illustrated with the reaction of society to the abdication of King Edward VIII. In 1936 King Edward VIII had to abdicate because he wanted to marry a divorcee. This abdication happened because society at that time believed that it would be dishonouring to the institution of marriage for the king to marry a divorcee. In contrast, modern society no longer has a high view of marriage and leaders are no longer expected to set godly examples. The current Prince of Wales has been told that he can become king despite the fact that he is married to a divorcee. This change of view about the sacredness of marriage has come about because of the relationship culture.

Notes

1 *The Daily Telegraph,* 7 April 2011.

IT IS FAR BETTER
TO LIVE A CELIBATE
SINGLE LIFE THAN TO
GO THROUGH LIFE
LURCHING FROM ONE
FAILED RELATIONSHIP
TO ANOTHER.

9. How the relationship culture undermines the single status

Key biblical principle: THE SINGLE STATUS IS GOOD (1 COR. 7:7)

The Bible teaches that the unmarried single status in which a person preserves his or her purity through celibacy is a good and honourable status. Paul said that he wished all men were like him (1 Cor. 7:7). One key advantage of the celibate single status is that a single person has more time to serve the Lord, because he or she does not have the distractions of marriage (1 Cor. 7:32–33). In past societies that followed biblical standards, to be single was a highly respected status. In past generations it was not uncommon for people to choose to live in chastity as bachelors or spinsters. Past societies honoured the single status and gave respect to it through various terms including 'bachelor', 'spinster' and 'Miss'. This culture was entirely in accord with biblical teaching. In contrast, modern society no longer gives honour to those who practise abstinence.

In my dealings with young people I have come across many examples of single people feeling under pressure to have relationships. Young single people are often told that what they need is a relationship and that it is strange if they are not looking for one. The pressure to have relationships is a new phenomenon that has come about because of the modern relationship culture. In the same way that the relationship culture has undermined the institution of marriage, so it has undermined the single status.

1. Modern society does not respect the celibate single status

Sadly, modern society no longer respects the celibate single status. It is expected that single people will be seeking to be in a relationship or to have casual sexual encounters, not to preserve their purity. The terms 'bachelor' and 'spinster' are no longer used because society no longer recognizes the single status as a worthy role. When someone declares that he or she is single, it is now assumed that this person has had relationships in the past and is in-between relationships. It is not assumed that he or she has chosen to be single as a lifelong choice.

2. Modern society has changed the meaning of the word 'single'

Modern society has confused the meaning of the word 'single' because it sometimes refers to someone who is promiscuous and casually dating different partners. Whereas being single used to mean having a pure celibate lifestyle with no sex and no relationships, now it can mean living a very promiscuous and immoral lifestyle.

3. Modern society does not regard virginity as a virtue

In past ages single people were assumed to be virgins if they were not widowed, and virginity was considered to be a noble thing for an adult who was unmarried. The apostle Paul referred to men who wanted to marry their 'virgin' (1 Cor. 7:36) because he assumed that the unmarried women were virgins. Queen Elizabeth I was known as the Virgin Queen because she was unmarried and therefore was assumed to be a virgin.

In modern society, it is no longer assumed that single people are virgins. And modern society no longer considers virginity to be a noble thing for an adult. The 2005 film *The 40-Year-Old Virgin* is so named because it is now considered remarkable and strange for a forty-year-old single person to be a virgin.

4. People are now defined by their sexuality, not by their marital status

Modern society no longer sees 'married' and 'single' as the two states of adult people. Instead people are now defined by their sexuality. People are labelled as 'heterosexual', 'homosexual', 'bisexual' or 'transsexual'. In Sodom and Gomorrah people would no doubt have been labelled in terms of their sexuality and not in terms of their marital status, so our society has gone the way of Sodom and Gomorrah in the way it labels people. When Christians see how the modern world uses language to promote its immoral standards, that again should be a strong motivation to avoid the relationship culture and its language.

5. Modern entertainment has virtually no single people as role models

Sadly, the entertainment industry does not portray a celibate single lifestyle as a positive lifestyle. There are very few role models who are prepared to be single for a long time before getting married. There are also few role models who want to spend their whole life as single people. Popular films like *Titanic* and *Pearl Harbor* are centred around characters who are seeking relationships and not around characters who are seeking to be single. When we consider the influence of the entertainment industry, it is no wonder that the single status is looked down upon in modern society.

In contrast to modern entertainment, romantic novels from past centuries contain role models who are happy to be single for their whole life or for a long period before getting married. In Jane Austen's *Mansfield Park*, Fanny Price is prepared to be single for a long time until Edmund proposes to her. In Charles Dickens's *David Copperfield*, Agnes is prepared to be single for a long period before marrying David Copperfield. In Elizabeth Gaskell's *North and South*, Miss Hale is single for a long period before finally marrying Mr Thornton.

6. There is pressure on single people to have relationships

The modern dating culture puts great pressure on single people to start having relationships. It is common to hear schoolgirls telling their friends, 'What you need is a boyfriend.' It is also common for people to be judged on their ability to attract a partner. Dating agencies have powerful marketing techniques, using questions like 'Do you need more love in your life?' This results in single people being made to feel inferior and abnormal. In reality, people who are single should feel very content with their status and not feel inferior to others.

Social networking sites such as Facebook add to the pressure on single people by having a place for people to declare their relationship status. The continual publication of a person's 'relationship status' gives the message that it is not good to be single. It also encourages people to be constantly monitoring everyone else's relationship status, which can make single people feel they are being judged.

7. Being single is better than having relationships

It is far better to live a celibate single life than to go through life lurching from one failed relationship to another. People do not always admit it, but going through serial relationships is often a miserable type of existence. People are on a continual roller-coaster of emotions and expectations. At one moment there is the possibility of settling down for life with a partner, then the relationship fails and there is disappointment and more emotional baggage. In contrast, people who remain single throughout life have great amounts of time to serve the Lord, as described in 1 Corinthians 7:32–33.

8. Single people can be greatly used by God

History shows that God has used single people in wonderful ways. The apostle Paul is one obvious example of an unmarried Christian who was used greatly by God. Other biblical examples of unmarried people of God include Elijah and Elisha in the Old Testament and John the Baptist in the New Testament.

Many missionaries have been unmarried Christians who have dedicated their lives in service for the Lord. Amy Carmichael (1867–1951) was an unmarried missionary in India who opened an orphanage and founded a mission. Mary Slessor (1848–1915) was another unmarried Christian who was a missionary in Nigeria. John Stott, who died in 2011 at the age of ninety, is an example of a recent well-known Christian who was single all his life. There are many single Christians today who are greatly used by God.

THE PROMISE THAT
GOD'S GRACE IS
SUFFICIENT IS ONE
THAT WE SHOULD
PARTICULARLY
REMEMBER IN
COURTSHIP.

10. Defending God's way for romance

Key biblical principle: STAND FIRM FOR BIBLICAL STANDARDS (1 COR. 16:13)

The Bible exhorts Christians to be watchful for spiritual battles and to stand firm for biblical truth. In our immoral age it is vital to stand firm for biblical teaching on marriage and sexual purity. The devil hates purity before marriage because it leads to stability and blessing for society and the church. The devil loves the relationship culture because it is damaging to marriage and causing a moral decline in society. It is vital for Christians to recognize that the devil is using the relationship culture to attack the institution of marriage and the church.

One of the key ways to judge a society is by how much it respects marriage and by the way people conduct themselves before marriage. Jesus said that His society was an 'adulterous generation' (Matt. 12:39). Because of the relationship culture we once again live in an adulterous generation that promotes sexual immorality. It is not easy to swim against the tide of ungodliness. However, following God's commands will lead to blessing for individuals and for the church.

1. Recognize the battle between two cultures

> The fear of the LORD is to hate evil (Prov. 8:13).

The main aspects of biblical standards of courtship and the modern relationship culture are summarized in the table overleaf to illustrate the important differences. Whereas the main purpose of biblical courtship is to investigate marriage, the main purpose of the modern relationship culture is to *have* a marriage-type relationship. A key aspect of the relationship culture is that it makes people think they have permission to have sexual intimacy if they are in a relationship. Some Christians today are making the mistake of thinking they can have sexual intimacy because they are 'in a relationship'. But there is absolutely no biblical reason for thinking that relationships give permission for sexual activity.

The table also summarizes the consequences of the two approaches to romance for individuals and society. Biblical courtship leads to many blessings and protection for individuals and society, whereas the relationship culture is the source of many harmful consequences, as can be seen so clearly in the world today.

Aspect	Biblically based courtship	Modern-day relationships
Origin	Biblical principles	Man's invention Entertainment industry
Purpose	Investigate marriage Make a choice Preserve purity	Have a type of marriage Love a choice Permission for sexual intimacy
Description	Friendship No official start End involves no split	Publicly recognized relationship Start officially announced End involves a split
How many? **How young?**	Not many courtships Start when old enough to marry	Many relationships before marriage Start at a very young age
View on marriage **View on parents**	High view of marriage Tendency to seek parental views	Low view of marriage Tendency not to seek parental views
Consequences for individuals	No pain of relationship splits Good preparation for marriage	Pain of relationship splits Poor preparation for marriage
Consequences for society	Marriage the norm Divorce uncommon Preservation of moral standards	Marriage in decline Divorce common Decline in moral standards

Main features of biblical courtship and the relationship culture

Christians are to hate evil (Prov. 8:13). In order to hate evil, it is first necessary to recognize evil, such as the evil of the relationship culture. It is important to realize that the relationship culture is an invention of modern society with the aim of rejecting biblical standards of courtship. It is important to recognize the fierce cultural battle between biblical standards and the modern relationship culture.

One of the reasons why Lot made the mistake of choosing to live in Sodom was because he did not recognize the evil of that place. That lack of discernment caused him to lower his moral standards, as illustrated when he offered his daughters to evil men. There are Christians today who cannot see the immorality of the relationship culture and who, like Lot, are adopting some of the immoral practices of the world.

The description of worldly desires in 1 John 2:15–16—'the lust of the flesh, the lust of the eyes, and the pride of life'—are very relevant to the relationship culture. Relationships involve the lust of the eyes because they often start with physical attraction and a desire for intimacy. Relationships involve the lust of the flesh because they promote lustful behaviour such as intimate kissing. Relationships involve pride because people are proud of their relationship status. Christians should therefore be very careful not to copy relationships from the world.

2. Recognize that the relationship culture can never work

In university campuses in the USA, sexual assault of women is so serious and widespread that some colleges are proposing that students sign contracts of consent before having sex. Such contracts may become essential in order for men to be able to prove they have not sexually assaulted a woman. Many people have said this will be impossible to implement in practice because most people will think that a contract is unnecessary and unromantic. But the fact that such bizarre proposals are being put forward shows how society has failed to make the relationship culture work.

When modern society looks at the harmful consequences of the relationship culture, it should conclude that intimate relationships do not work and cannot work. It should also conclude that the Bible is right to command that there should be purity before marriage. However, the world is not prepared to give up its goal of having sexual freedom. Modern society believes that the problems of the relationship culture can be solved with better education. However, sex education such as Sex and Relationships Education (SRE) will always be doomed to failure because it is based on the unbiblical idea that there can be sexual freedom outside of marriage without harmful consequences.

When Christians consider how the relationship culture is harmful and cannot work, surely that should motivate them to avoid that culture. And when Christians consider how Western society has rejected a biblical courtship culture that was good for society and protected women and girls, surely that should encourage Christians to follow biblical standards of courtship.

3. Exceed the righteousness of the best non-Christians

> For I say to you, that unless your righteousness exceeds the righteousness of the scribes and Pharisees, you will by no means enter the kingdom of heaven (Matt. 5:20).

A Christian is called to have a righteousness that exceeds that of religious and morally upright people. Christians today should be aiming to meet and exceed the standards of people from previous generations who saved themselves for marriage. If Christians from Jane Austen's time were here today, they would no doubt find the relationship culture very immoral. Even many non-Christians from previous eras would find the relationship culture immoral. There are also many cultures around the world today that advocate purity in courtship. Christians should aim to exceed the standards of such cultures in the area of courtship.

It is wrong to think that God simply wants Christians to have better relationships than non-Christians in the current culture. Lot tried to be better than the world when he offered his daughters to the promiscuous crowd. While he was better than the world in which he lived, what he did was still very immoral.

There are Christians today who make the mistake of trying to justify their romantic relationships on the basis that they are a little better than those of the world today. Some Christians claim that, if there is selflessness and faithfulness in intimate relationships, this makes them morally acceptable. However, Christians are called to flee sexual immorality, not to indulge in a sexual immorality that has a supposed degree of selflessness and faithfulness.

4. Seek parental advice

Since single people are subject to their parents until marriage (Gen. 2:24), it is right that they seek advice from their parents about marriage. Parents are usually the people who know their children better than anyone else, so their opinions are very valuable even if they are not Christians. Before going out with someone, therefore, it is a good thing to discuss the appropriateness and wisdom of that decision with your parents.

In past centuries respect was shown to parents in the way a man would ask a woman's father if he could court her. While it is not always appropriate today to ask a woman's father for permission to go out with her, it is still important for a man to show respect to a woman's father by protecting the purity of the woman and by not forming a marriage-like relationship that would diminish the parent–child relationship.

5. Give guidance to young people

Parents and church leaders have an important role to play in helping young people follow biblical standards of courtship. Advice can be given on areas such as standards of dress, choice of entertainment and choice of friends. Practical measures can also be taken to help young people avoid temptation. One example is not to let them meet with a member of the opposite sex in a private room such as a bedroom. In his book *Her Hand in Marriage*,[1] Douglas Wilson argues that fathers in particular have a duty to protect the purity of their daughters.

Modern communications technology makes it very easy for children to have secret friendships. Therefore, Christian parents should be proactive in monitoring what goes on with mobile phones and computers and should apply restrictions such as banning their use during the night. A recent craze among young people is to send pictures of themselves naked or semi-naked to their boyfriend/girlfriend using their mobile phone (sexting). It is important for parents to be aware that children from Christian families can be drawn into such practices.

The police often say that parents need to be more aware of whom their children are talking to online because of the dangers of their being abused and led astray. The reason why the police make this plea is because many parents do not know what their children are doing on the Internet and on their mobile phones.

6. Seek God's help

God knows the peer pressure Christians face to conform to the relationship culture. And God is ready and able to help Christians resist that temptation. When Christians seek God's help and trust in His Word they will be helped to follow the right path. There are several ways a Christian can seek help from God and His Word. Some of the following points have been described already in this book, but they are repeated here because they are so important.

The psalmist spoke of how he loved God's commands exceedingly (Ps. 119:167) and how he was in awe of God's Word (119:161). It is helpful to nurture a love and respect for God's commands because it is easier to obey something we love and respect. So it is good to remember God's commands, such as to abstain from sexual immorality (Acts 15:20) and to honour marriage (Heb. 13:4).

It is important for a Christian to pray for the fruit of the Spirit, especially for self-control, faithfulness and patience (Gal. 5:22–23). Self-control is needed to obey the command to abstain from sexual immorality. Faithfulness is needed because there should be faithfulness to a future spouse. Patience is needed because a Christian should be prepared to wait until marriage for the pleasures of marriage.

The promise that God's grace is sufficient is one that we should particularly remember in courtship (2 Cor. 12:9). We should also remember that God does not allow us to be tempted beyond what we can bear (1 Cor. 10:13). Such promises show that God can strengthen a Christian to withstand temptation.

It is helpful to remember the important biblical promise that God honours those who honour Him by faith and obedience (1 Sam. 2:30). Often that will mean God providing a spouse and a happy marriage, but even if marriage does not happen, God will still honour that godly conduct. God knows what is best for us and He is faithful to bless those who follow His commands.

7. Walk by faith

Finding a spouse is a key area where a person needs to walk by faith, not by sight (2 Cor. 5:7). Following biblical standards of courtship involves faith because they involve a person being prepared to wait until marriage for the pleasures of marriage. Avoiding relationships involves the faith that God will provide a spouse.

In contrast, relationships involve walking by sight because decisions are made for short-term pleasures.

8. Choose God's way for romance, not the world's way

The table on the next page summarizes biblical teaching on romance (with some key Bible texts) and contrasts this with the false teaching of the world. God has designed marriage as the only way for romantic fulfilment and sexual intimacy. However, modern society believes that marriage is not sacred and that there can be romantic fulfilment and sexual intimacy outside of marriage. The Bible teaches that divorce and separation are traumatic and against God's plan. However, modern society believes splitting up is normal and necessary. The Bible warns there are harmful consequences to sexual immorality. However, modern society believes there are no inherent dangers in sex outside of marriage. It is vital for Christians to recognize the false teaching of the world and not to follow the relationship culture.

There is a choice: the biblically based way of courtship or the man-made relationship culture; saving yourself for marriage or having marital pleasures now; godliness or sexual immorality; caution or haste; safety or danger; purity or baggage; a stable life or a broken life; doing what is good for the institution of marriage or doing what damages the institution of marriage; doing what is good for society or doing what damages society; and doing what is good for the church or doing what damages the church.

The battle for purity in courtship is a vital spiritual battle in the church today. There is an urgent need for God's people to choose the way of biblical standards of courtship.

Notes

1 **Douglas Wilson,** *Her Hand in Marriage: Biblical Courtship in the Modern World* (Moscow, ID: Canon Press, 1997).

Biblical teaching	False teaching of the world
Romantic fulfilment is found only in marriage (Gen. 2:24)	Romance can be fulfilling outside of marriage
Marriage is sacred (Heb. 13:4) and therefore there can be no relationship status (Gen. 2:24)	Marriage is not sacred and therefore there can be an alternative relationship status
All sexual intimacy outside of marriage is immoral (Heb. 13:4)	Being in a relationship gives permission for sexual intimacy
Being one flesh should happen only in marriage (Gen. 2:24)	Being in a relationship joins two people together as one
Separation is traumatic and against God's plan (Mal. 2:16)	'Splitting up' is necessary and something to get used to
Illicit relationships have harmful consequences (Prov. 5–7)	There are no inherent harmful consequences to relationships
It is important to stay pure before marriage (Prov. 31:12; Deut. 22)	It is not important to think of the feelings of a future spouse
The relationship culture can never work (Prov. 5–7; Mal. 2:16; Heb. 13:4)	The relationship culture can be made to work with enough education

Biblical teaching on romance versus the world's teaching